Golf Wales

where to play, eat and stay

GRAFFEG

Published by Graffeg
First published 2007
Copyright © Graffeg 2007
ISBN 9781905582020

Graffeg, Radnor Court, 256 Cowbridge Road
East, Cardiff CF5 1GZ Wales UK.
Tel: +44(0)29 2037 7312
sales@graffeg.com www.graffeg.com
Graffeg are hereby identified as the authors
of this work in accordance with section 77
of the Copyrights, Designs and Patents
Act 1988.

Distributed by the Welsh Books Council
www.cllc.org.uk
castellbrychan@cllc.org.uk

A CIP Catalogue record for this book is
available from the British Library.

Designed and produced by
Peter Gill & Associates
sales@petergill.com
www.petergill.com

Map base information reproduced by
permission of Ordnance Survey on behalf of
HMSO © Crown Copyright (2007).
All rights reserved. Ordnance Survey
Licence number 100020518

Golf Wales Written by John Hopkins,
foreword by Ian Woosnam, where to eat and
stay by Colin Pressdee.

The author and publisher would like to
thank the golf clubs featured in this book,
who generously gave their advice and time
to the author. Also thanks to Rob Holt,
Ryder Cup Wales and to Claire Sanders,
Visit Wales / Welsh Assembly Government
for their advice and encouragement. Thank
you to the Visit Wales Image Centre for
supplying us with outstanding images of
some of the top courses in Wales.

The publishers are also grateful to the
Welsh Books Council for their financial
support and marketing advice.
www.gwales.com

Every effort has been made to ensure that
the information in this book is current and
it is given in good faith at the time of
publication. Please be aware that
circumstances can change and be sure to
check details before making travel plans.

Tenovus the cancer charity:
A donation of 40p for each book sold will be
made to Tenovus the cancer charity
(registered charity number 1054015).
Tenovus is one of the UK's leading cancer
charities and the chosen charity of Ryder
Cup Wales 2010 Limited. The charity funds
first class cancer research, patient care
services, and education and prevention
programmes. Anyone wanting information
or with a concern about cancer can contact
the Tenovus Freephone Cancer Helpline on
0808 808 1010. Tenovus the cancer charity,
43 The Parade, Cardiff, CF24 3AB,
telephone 029 2048 2000 and website
tenovus.com

Golf
Wales

where to play, eat and stay

GRAFFEG

Ian Woosnam

Foreword

I am very pleased to have the opportunity to write this Foreword because it can only help focus attention on Wales in the build-up to the 2010 Ryder Cup and make the country's courses better known to a wider audience. I, in common with so many others, believe that Wales is the undiscovered golfing destination. There are so many good golf courses that people have only heard of; so many they have never played. If this book causes a flurry of enquiries at golf clubs in Wales, then great.

Writing this Foreword allows me to reflect on what being Welsh means to me, what Wales stands for and what we have to offer as a country. I remember playing all these courses and the memories take me back to when it all started. Would I have won the US Masters in 1991 had I been born in another country? Would I have become the world number one, won 44 professional tournaments around the world and been honoured with the captaincy of the European Ryder Cup Team? The realistic answer to these questions is, "who knows?" What I do know is that there can be no doubt about my Welshness, my enthusiasm for that country and respect for its heritage. I am Welsh from top to toe.

In 1995 I wrote the Foreword to the book commemorating the Centenary of the Welsh Golfing Union. Part of what I wrote is as valid now as it was then: "Although I was born in the village of St Martins, near Oswestry, on the English side of the border between England and Wales, that does not make me English. Nor does the fact that I grew up playing golf at Llanymynech, where three holes are in England and 15 in Wales, take away from the pride I have in pulling on the red sweater of Wales. I regard

I have said many times publicly and privately that captaining Europe in the Ryder Cup at the K Club near Dublin in 2006 was the biggest week of my life.

myself as a Welshman through and through, as did Lloyd George, the Liberal prime minister, who was born in Manchester."

Watching my team equal the record margin of victory and win all five series of matches made me very proud of them.

I have said many times publicly and privately that captaining Europe in the Ryder Cup at the K Club near Dublin in 2006 was the biggest week of my life. Watching my team equal the record margin of victory and win all five series of matches made me very proud of them. It was the hardest week of my life but also the best. I am sure that officials from Wales were there absorbing information to put to use at Celtic Manor in 2010. They have seen what they have to follow but I have no doubt, based on the success of their bid and the progress to date, that Wales and Celtic Manor will be up to the challenge.

Hope you enjoy the book.

John Hopkins

I hurtle around a lot...

I hurtle to and from airports, to and from interviews. I get off a plane and hurtle towards the car hire desk ready to hurtle through the countryside to my next golf tournament, except when I am in Dublin and there is a half hour wait at the Hertz desk. Hurtle, hurtle, hurtle. Even my writing could sometimes be described as hurtling to get the words down in time to meet a deadline. "John, you're the page lead on page 84. Let us have 700 words by 6.30 please." Sentences like that make me hurtle.

I do not hurtle when I am on a golf course, however. I may have done so to get there on time, may be doing so to get back to my hotel or home after it, but when I am on the course I try to create an atmosphere of anything but hurtling. Hurtling may be good for moving quickly. Hurtling is bad for golf.

Early in 2006 I met Peter Gill, the publisher of this book, at a party given by my friends Tony and Maggie Fletcher. Quickly the idea of a book came up and I was provided with an opportunity to stop hurtling around for a while and to write about my favourite courses in Wales. A few months later The Times asked me to do a short piece about my ten best courses in Britain and Ireland. What do you mean by best?"I asked. "Do you mean my hardest, my most enjoyable, those with the biggest names?" They could not reply.

When I talk of my favourite golf courses in Wales, I mean those I like the most for a number of different reasons; those that bring a smile of affection to my face. They do not have to be inordinately long – though some are – nor do they have to be easy on the eye –

When I talk of my favourite golf courses in Wales, I mean those I like the most for a number of different reasons; those that bring a smile of affection to my face.

though, again, some are – nor terribly difficult – though they can be. It is not essential that they are near the sea, though most are. They are a combination of the most enjoyable and the most demanding, the prettiest, most fun to play courses in the Principality. And they are all 18 holes.

I really enjoy the nine-hole course at Newport in Pembrokeshire where I play each August and I think that the 6th is a wonderful par 3 from the back tee with the wind in your face. Nearly 190 yards to a sliver of a green set slightly at an angle among dunes. >

Perhaps the green is too small for that length of shot but even when played at its more normal length it remains a testing short hole, visually satisfying. But I had enough difficulty in winnowing down 18 or 20 of my favourite courses, without introducing the added complication of including a nine-holer.

I am a member of Royal Porthcawl, which I believe has the most atmospheric clubhouse in the world, one that is nearer to the sea than almost any other. It has an outstanding practice ground where I can (and often do) lose myself to the accompaniment of birdsong and a charming professional in Peter Evans, who talks sensibly and calmly about the myriad complications of this wretched game. Choosing Royal Porthcawl to be amongst my favourites was not difficult.

I am a member of Royal Porthcawl, which I believe has the most atmospheric clubhouse in the world

In pursuit of some of the others, I relived my childhood. For a few months in the summer of 2006, I revisited and played Royal St David's, where I had competed in the Welsh Boys' Championship in the early Sixties. I went back to Nefyn, where I had played as a child. I stood on the tee of the old 10th on the old inward nine holes and I shut my eyes and remembered how fearsome I had found the drive from that tee. Cliff top to the right, road to the left and a ribbon of fairway in between, a ribbon that diminished every time you looked at it. It was a daunting tee shot.

Likewise, I worried about getting my second shot on the 10th up the bank. I used to think I would thin it and my ball would roll slowly

I got my first irons, a 7 and 9 iron made by John Letters and stamped with the name of Fred Daly, who had won the Open in 1947. I was prouder of them than I would have been if I'd been given the Mona Lisa.

back, perhaps to my feet. Then there was the tee shot up to the old 12th, no more than 110 yards. Was I sure I could flick the ball high enough and get it to stop on a green the size of a postage stamp? I was a much better player as a boy than I am now but I have far less fear of that drive on the 10th now and the tee shot to the 12th than I did then. Funny that. I think it is something to do with physically growing up.

The first golf strokes I hit were on Stinchcombe Hill in Gloucestershire. Born a left-hander, I soon found there were no children's clubs for southpaws. My father turned me round and some years after that I got my first irons, a 7 and 9 iron made by John Letters and stamped with the name of Fred Daly, who had won the Open in 1947. I was prouder of them than I would have been if I'd been given the Mona Lisa.

Half of the excitement the clubs gave me was created by the anticipation of getting them. They were ordered when we were at home but had not arrived by the time we embarked on a family holiday to North Wales. So they were diverted to Dros-Y-Mor, the holiday house on wooden stilts we rented in a little bay next to Porthdinllaen. The pattern of most days was the same. I would gobble down my breakfast and make my way to the golf club where I would sit and talk with Dennis Grace, the professional, or practise. At lunchtime I would return home. One morning I was descending the cliff top path when something made me look up at Dros-Y-Mor and there was my mother out on the veranda, waving furiously. My clubs had arrived.

So many things have happened to me in Wales. For a few years I went to the Cathedral School in Llandaff. Not much golf then but plenty >

of rugby. I met my wife by the side of the 13th at Royal Porthcawl golf club. I played in two Welsh Boys' Championships at Llandrindod Wells about which John V Moody wrote 800 words daily in the *Western Mail*, and I played in one championship at Royal St David's. For some years I was rugby correspondent of *The Sunday Times* and used to cover Wales in the Five Nations and would often write features about the leading players. And then I switched to golf and found myself in Wales again, this time at Porthcawl for the Amateur Championship, say, or Ashburnham for the Home Internationals.

As I travelled around reinspecting my favourite courses for this book, I was reminded again and again of conversations I have had and no doubt will continue to have with golfers who want to come to Britain. "Where should we play?" they ask, or, "ten of us are coming for a golfing holiday in Ireland. What will it be like in September? Do you have any short cuts we should take, any insider's advice?"

And I think to myself: come to Wales. We'll show you a good time.

I take a deep breath and answer their questions as best I can, all the time thinking: why don't they come to Wales? I think of the tourists who fly in to Heathrow and head for the Home Counties, those who arrive at Manchester and make for the Lancashire coast, those who land at Prestwick or Edinburgh or Dublin. And I think to myself: come to Wales. We'll show you a good time.

Imagine Aberdovey on a summer's evening. Think of Nefyn when a light wind is blowing across the peninsula. Conwy in a wind is a test for anyone, as is Royal St David's crouched down beneath the castle.

If there is one thing I want this book to do it is to convey my enjoyment and pleasure at playing golf in Wales.

Southerndown, Royal Porthcawl and Pyle and Kenfig are a cracking trio of courses. The 16th at Machynys is a terrific hole. Tenby is fun, Ashburnham long. So it goes on.

Three years to the Ryder Cup.

Wake up to Wales as a golfing destination.

I hope this book helps to do that.

If there is one thing I want this book to do it is to convey my enjoyment and pleasure at playing golf in Wales. Some years ago my friend and colleague Peter Corrigan wrote about Wales, calling the country a hidden golfing destination and describing some of the golf courses as hidden gems. He was dead right. There are many really good courses in Wales that are relatively undiscovered. It is time to spread the word. Shout it from the rooftops. Three years to the Ryder Cup. Wake up to Wales as a golfing destination. I hope this book helps to do that. ●

Ian Woosnam, winning Ryder Cup Captain 2006.

contents

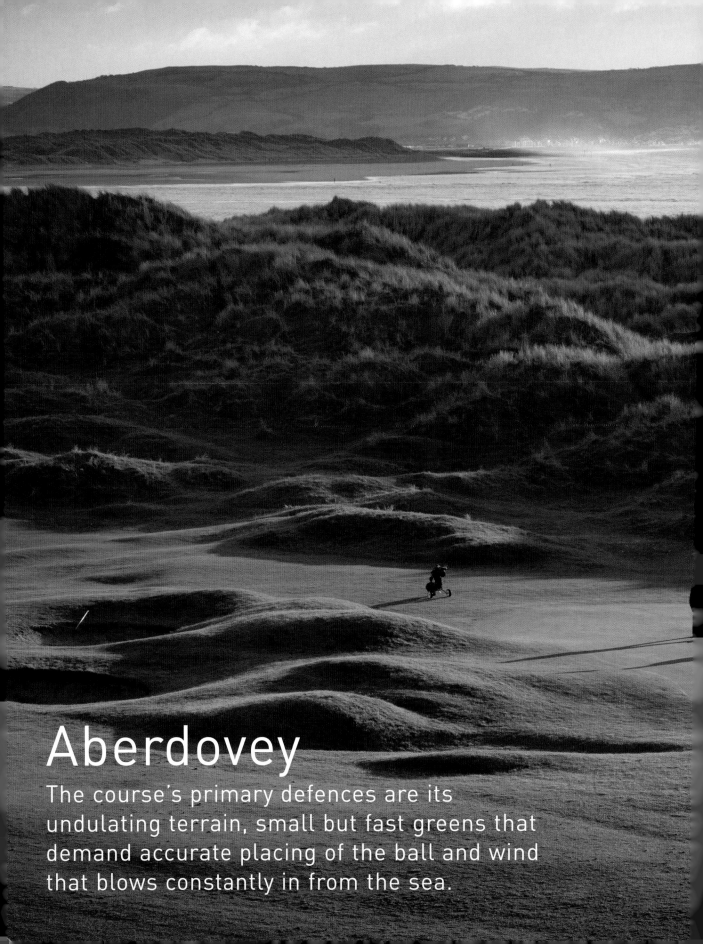

Aberdovey

The course's primary defences are its undulating terrain, small but fast greens that demand accurate placing of the ball and wind that blows constantly in from the sea.

Aberdovey Golf Club
18 hole, Par 71 (6,454 yds)
Links course.

Patric Dickinson, the writer came up with a sound piece of advice for anyone thinking of putting pen to paper about Aberdovey. "If one dare write about Aberdovey at all, one must begin by letting Bernard Darwin through on the way to the 1st tee," Dickinson wrote. This was a felicitous reference to the Darwin connection with Aberdovey, which is as strong as a steel hawser. An uncle of his, Colonel Richard Ruck, later to become Major-General Sir Richard, is said to have used flower pots borrowed from a woman in the village and cut holes in the land in which to put them to lay out the course. Aberdovey was where Darwin spent many summer holidays and where the young Darwin won the first club tournament, in April 1892, with a gross score of 100. He was completely besotted by the place and wrote once: "About this one course in the world, I am a hopeless and shameful sentimentalist and I glory in my shame."

...at the mouth of the estuary of the River Dovey in the midst of Cardigan Bay, a gorgeous position...

Although a number of courses owe something of their historical being to the railways, none does so quite as much as Aberdovey. Even its most ardent supporters would admit it is not exactly the easiest place in the world to get to. It's in mid-Wales, at the mouth of the estuary of the River Dovey in the midst of Cardigan Bay, a gorgeous position but one that even today, in the day of the e-mail, the ipod and the BlackBerry, can take an inordinate length of time to reach. For years there was really only one way to get there and that was to let the train take the strain.

In 1995, to mark the centenary of the founding of the Welsh Golfing Union, I recreated for *The Times* a journey Darwin had

made from London to mid-Wales and had written about in one of the incomparable essays for which he was rightly famous. Darwin wrote of arriving at Euston by cab, of tipping a porter sixpence and of taking a corner seat in a carriage, of having arrived "absurdly early".

I did the same and caught a train that, I noted, duly began to move unenthusiastically towards the Midlands. "The stations will whirl past," Darwin wrote and they did for me too until Birmingham New Street where a screen on platform 7B showed that the Aberystwyth train left at 14.07. At the bottom of the screen were the words Regional Railways, a less mellifluous name than The Cambrian Railway, three words that so excited Darwin.

We passed through any number of places until, as Darwin put it, "the train comes into a country of mountains and jolly foaming mountain streams. It pants up the steep hill to the solitary little station called Talerddig." And after that to Machynlleth – "let a Saxon try to pronounce that!" Darwin wrote – before reaching >

Left: Bernard Darwin, who has done more than anyone to publicise Aberdovey.

Above: River Dovey estuary

• • • • • • • • • • • • • • •

Aberdovey where "there is a wild rush of small boys outside our carriage window, fighting and clamouring for the privilege of carrying one's clubs. *Nunc dimittis* – we have arrived at Aberdovey."

Golf at Aberdovey, as it is at Tenby, is a reminder of what the game was like in a bygone era...

In the early 1900s one of those youths jostling for Darwin's bag may well have been the son of the club pro. Harry Cooper would later accompany his father to the US, acquire the nickname "Light Horse" for the speed at which he played, and gain a reputation as one of the best players never to win a major championship. Cooper lost a playoff with Tommy Armour for the 1927 US Open and settled for second place at the 1936 US Open.

When you arrive at the station these days, there is no rush of young boys to carry one's clubs, but in many ways what Darwin saw when he got off that train a century ago is the same scene as greets a present-day visitor. The 18th green is only a chip shot away from the clubhouse, the 1st tee and the railway line. Many tees adjoin the greens of previous holes, as they do on the Old Course at St Andrews.

Golf at Aberdovey, as it is at Tenby, is a reminder of what the game was like in a bygone era, a time before noisy earthmovers scraped and shaped the landscape, and long before water and waste bunkers and artificial grassy mounds were considered an essential element of a course's defences. The holes go more or less straight out and straight back on land between the railway line and the sea and it lies beneath bare, brooding mountains >

Right: Putting out on the
13th green on a typically
breezy day.

ABERDOVEY G.C.

13	PAR	YDS	SI
	5	539	1
	5	496	1

on which hill farmers graze their sheep. It is as close if not closer to the sea than Ashburnham and Harlech and like them there is a constant murmur from the sea yet very few glimpses of it.

Aberdovey measures 6,454 yards from the back tees and includes three par 5s and four par 3s, three of them on the outward nine.

Aberdovey measures 6,454 yards from the back tees and includes three par 5s and four par 3s, three of them on the outward nine. One of those par 3s, the 173-yard 3rd known as Cader, was Darwin's favourite short hole. It requires a blind tee shot to a green that in the writer's day was surrounded by sand. Darwin said: "....the club is rather proud of this ....hole, which consists of a rather terrifying iron shot perfectly blind over a vast and formidable hill shored up with black railway sleepers onto a little green oasis amid a desert of sand."

Above: Path to 13th tee.

The course's primary defences are its undulating terrain, small but fast greens that demand accurate placing of the ball and wind that blows constantly in from the sea. The holes alter in character like a piece of music: the opening ones are quiet, some by the sea, some down in the central plain; the middle holes grow bolder and from the 12th onward they become downright frenzied. Just stand on the tee of the 288-yard 16th with an onshore crosswind and see if you can find the narrow fairway. "No man is a medal winner until he has played that shot and sees the ball lying safely on the turf," Darwin wrote. And having reached the sanctuary of the fairway, are you accurate enough to find the shelf of a green with a sharp drop off to the left and sand dunes to the right?

Even if you par this tricky little devil, can you do the same at the 17th and 18th, both stout par 4s that require pinpoint driving and approach play? The 18th, say the locals with an admirable degree of bias, is perhaps the best finishing hole in Welsh golf, with the railway running down the left and ditches and bunkers on the right.

Harlech and Royal St David's is only a short train ride away. So is Barmouth. And Bernard Darwin is never far away, or so it seems. His presence seeps out of the walls of the clubhouse and an old man resembling Darwin guides you around the course. His ghost is waving at you as you leave, as it was welcoming you when you arrived, had you but known it. Remember to wave back. ●

On the 3rd tee, with the hills of
Ceredigion across the estuary,
you could almost be the only
golfer in the world.

Ashburnham

Few clubs can match Ashburnham's length –
from the back tees it is very nearly 7,000 yards –
and few its achievement of having three Ryder
Cup captains win a tournament on their course.

Ashburnham Golf Club
18 hole, Par 72 (6,624 yds)
Links course.

1995 was an important year for golf in Wales. To mark the centenary of the founding of the Welsh Golfing Union, the Walker Cup was held at Royal Porthcawl. Purely in the cause of chauvinism it is worth noting that the Welsh Golfing Union was founded on 11 January 1895, 25 and 29 years respectively before its counterparts in Scotland and England. You may remember the Walker Cup? Some chap named Woods was a member of the US team that lost to a Great Britain and Ireland team captained by Clive Brown, a Welshman. Whatever happened to him? Woods, I mean, not Brown. Probably living quietly somewhere in the US tending his asparagus.

Yet more than most clubs it feels like a house, or, actually, two that have been joined together, and a warm and welcoming one at that.

In the summer of 1994, the Home Internationals were held at Ashburnham and one afternoon I was standing with Peter McEvoy, the England captain, out by the 4th hole when a long-legged Englishman with a fresh face and a quick swing went past. "David Howell," McEvoy said quietly as if I had not recognised one of the heroes of the Walker Cup. "I think he's got it all. He's quite long and there is something about him. He could go all the way."

Those words came to mind when I revisited Ashburnham recently. As usual I found myself lost within moments of arriving. The clubhouse is unlike most clubhouses where the locker rooms are as easy to find as the bars. At Ashburnham you walk in through one door, push open another and find yourself somewhere you don't want to be. You turn left again, go round another corner and

the door in front of you leads out of the clubhouse. You go up the stairs and find the lavatories, crash into another door marked Private and so it goes. Yet more than most clubs it feels like a house, or, actually, two that have been joined together, and a warm and welcoming one at that. And as for its collection of memorabilia, that is among the best in Wales.

At Ashburnham you walk in through one door, push open another and find yourself somewhere you don't want to be. You turn left again, go round another corner and the door in front of you leads out of the clubhouse.

Few clubs can match Ashburnham's length – from the back tees it is very nearly 7,000 yards – and few its achievement of having three Ryder Cup captains win a tournament on their course. They are Dai Rees and the 1959 PGA Championship, Bernard Gallacher and the 1969 Schweppes PGA tournament and Sam Torrance and the 1976 Martini International tournament. >

Above: On a clear day, startling views of Rhossili Bay, Gower, are visible from the clubhouse.

Some other interesting facts about Ashburnham:

- although it is by the sea it is like Aberdovey in that the sea can only be seen from the 1st and 16th tees;

- it takes its name from the fifth Earl of Ashburnham who once owned the land and became the club's first President in 1894;

- the old clubhouse used to be in the Ashburnham Hotel where Amelia Earhart spent a night after landing in Burry Port at the end of her historic trans-Atlantic solo flight. The old artisan clubhouse used to be in "The Ship Aground" pub, no more than a decent drive from the clubhouse;

- in the nearby Pembrey churchyard German pilots who were shot down during the Second World War are buried alongside Napoleon's niece;

- the oldest inter-club competition in Wales is for the Tenby Putter. It is competed for annually by Tenby and Ashburnham golf clubs. It started in 1895;

- the best downstairs view of the course is from the bay window
  in the Ladies' lounge. From the balcony upstairs, the view isn't
  half bad either.

in the nearby Pembrey churchyard German pilots who were
shot down during the Second World War are buried
alongside Napoleon's niece.

What is noticeable about the course the moment the visitor steps
out on to the putting green is a grassy bank that runs across it.
It was once the route for the colliery railway carrying coal to
Pembrey port. The 1st, a par 3, the 16th, another par 3, and the
18th, a dog leg par 4, are all this side of the bank on a rather
pinched piece of land. The remaining 15 holes are the other side.
Ashburnham and Royal Lytham are among the very few courses
that start with a par 3.

Founded as a nine-hole course in 1894, the course was extended
by J.H. Taylor, one of The Great Triumvirate, before the First >

Above: Pembrey church
breaking the skyline in the
distance beyond the clubhouse.

• • • • • • • • • • • • • • World War and modified again in 1923 by F.H. Hawtree. In an echo of what Bernard Darwin said about Aberdovey, Harry Vardon, another of The Great Triumvirate, played it twice, once with James Braid, the third member of The Great Triumvirate, and declared it was the course in Wales he liked best.

Get past the 2nd and there is a change of direction as the holes turn to run westward, one after another. This is where the course really begins. From the 3rd to the 9th are two par 5s, three par 4s and one par 3. To the right is scrub and land that the club owns but has not yet been able to bring into play. To the left are dunes which later give way to the incoming holes.

Harry Vardon, another of The Great Triumvirate, played it twice, once with James Braid, the third member of The Great Triumvirate, and declared it was the course in Wales he liked best.

Around the turn are two of my favourite holes. The 8th is a double dog leg, going from right to left at the start before changing from left to right near the end. The 9th goes in almost the opposite direction and curls from right to left with a green half hidden behind a grassy shoulder. To the left the green is waisted with a bunker narrowing the putting surface. On the 11th there is what appears from a distance to be a gibbet. It is in fact a bell.

The 12th seems rather like the 9th in its shape though it is 40 yards shorter and downwind might be drivable, though only for the long hitters. The 13th is a par 3 that turns toward the west >

Right: The Gower Peninsula is clearly visible across the Loughor estuary.

The long, thin 14th green is protected by dunes and has a hint of mystery about it.

again and the tee of the 14th, a shortish, risk/reward par 5, provides a good vantage spot from which to watch play on the 3rd, 4th and 13th. The long, thin 14th green is protected by dunes and has a hint of mystery about it.

The distant clubhouse is visible from the 15th tee, which snuggles down beneath a dune from the top of which is a memorable view. There is room behind this tee for expansion, though the area into which such expansion would intrude is a Site of Special Scientific Interest and thus tightly controlled. There were once plans to move the clubhouse out to this part of the course but that idea foundered, too. "We have a duty of care that we take very seriously," Ian Church, the general manager, said. "We own the land to the right of the course on the way out too and to the right of the 14th and 15th on the way in. This is a blessing and a responsibility I take seriously. To do anything will take vision, a degree of calculated risk and cash. It's my function to put the club in the position of having all three." ●

Left: The 14th green may be a safe par 5, but it is a classic risk/reward birdie hole.

Celtic Manor

One of the biggest resorts in Europe with its three golf courses and two hotels.

Celtic Manor Resort

Montgomerie Course – 18 hole, Par 69 (6,369 yds) Parkland course.

Roman Road – 18 hole, Par 70 (6,495 yds) Parkland course.

Ryder Cup Course – 18 hole, Par 71 (7,459 yds) Parkland course.

Drive west on the M4 from Heathrow or Reading or Bristol and only a few minutes after you have crossed the Severn Bridge you will see Celtic Manor rear up on your right hand side. It is almost impossible to miss, towering as it does over the motorway. It is a monument to the success of Sir Terry Matthews, a Welshman who was born in a maternity hospital on that site 60 years ago, a man who lives in Canada and does not play golf.

It is a monument to the success of Sir Terry Matthews, a Welshman who was born in a maternity hospital on that site 60 years ago, a man who lives in Canada and does not play golf.

It was Matthews, above all others, who got the 2010 Ryder Cup to Wales. Tony Lewis, the engaging and articulate Welshman, led the team that did the negotiations and made the presentations. But it was Matthews, Wales's richest man, whose considerable wealth comes from the electronics industry, whose backing of the bid made it more acceptable to the Ryder Cup Committee when it was searching for a venue for 2010 than those of the Scottish applicants, Gleneagles, Turnberry, Loch Lomond and Carnoustie.

Top: The Ryder Cup which will be at stake here in 2010.

Opposite: The two tier driving range at the Golf Academy.

Left: Relaxing in the Forum.

Right: Looking down into the hotel's striking atrium.

There are few more historic sites on which golf courses have been built in Wales – or anywhere else for that matter. Though you might not know it, the Romans seem to have been everywhere in these parts a couple of millennia ago. In his informative book, *The Golfers Guide to Wales*, John Pinner, the golf writer, explains that "Caerleon, a driver and a five iron from Celtic Manor, was once one of the most famous towns in Britain. Once known by the Latin name Isca Silurum, it was the capital >

town and headquarters of the Roman legions that inhabited Wales. Remains of the amphitheatre can still be seen...."

It is where the 2010 Ryder Cup will be staged and thus images of it will be flashed around the world in September 2010.

Not all of the history is contributed by the Romans, though they did build a road known as Via Julia to their fortress at Caerleon and still visible to this day is a site of a Roman gladiator training school. Via Julia runs through the resort and the Robert Trent Jones-designed Roman Road course is named after it. The Celtic Manor Wales Open was held on the Roman Road course in 2005 and 2006. At that event in June 2006 Phil Archer stood over a seven-foot putt knowing that if he holed it he would go round in 59, the first time 60 had been broken on the highest level of the European Tour. He missed.

There are two other courses at Celtic Manor. The first of these

two is The Montgomerie, designed by Colin Montgomerie, who casts a long shadow over Celtic Manor and has already had a considerable attachment to the resort. The Montgomerie comprises nine holes from the old Wentwood Hills course that were not needed for the Ryder Cup course and the back nine of The Montgomerie is built on land which previously housed the Coldra Woods 18-hole Academy course. The second of these two courses is the one that will make Celtic Manor's name, if it needs any making. It is where the 2010 Ryder Cup will be staged and thus images of it will be flashed around the world in September 2010. At the time of writing it was known simply as the Ryder Cup course though it was thought that this would change in time.

The Ryder Cup course can extend to nearly 7,500 yards and offers testing holes that make their way in a series of squiggles along the floor of the valley. There is water everywhere. They are visually stunning and technically difficult. Those spectators at the Ryder Cup who take up positions on the left of the closing holes will feel much as spectators might have done in a Roman amphitheatre all those years ago. They will be able to watch >

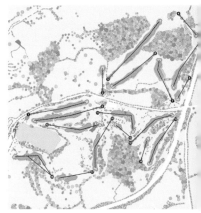

Left: 11th hole on the Montgomerie Course.

Top: Colin Montgomerie playing an approach shot to a green at the 2006 Celtic Manor Wales Open.

Above: Montgomerie Course plan.

Not what you would normally see behind a tee. Miguel Angel Jiménez, watched by Ian Woosnam, is not distracted by the artwork as he tees off during the 2006 Celtic Manor Wales Open.

● ● ● ● ● ● ● ● ● ● ● ● ● ● ● ● competitors play each of the last three holes without moving from their viewing eyries. There has not been a Ryder Cup venue where that can be said and there promises to be a special atmosphere over this part of the course as the matches reach their conclusions each day.

It is a matter of some pride to those at Celtic Manor that its three courses offer three different challenges.

You can't miss Celtic Manor, a boisterous sort of place that sprawls over 1,400 acres. Just as it dominates views northwards from the M4, so its height and commanding position provide spectacular views across the Severn to Somerset and Devon and towards the Brecon Beacons to the north. No one visits it and remains unmoved by its scale. It is one of the biggest resorts in Europe and as well as its three golf courses it has two hotels. The smaller of the two is the Manor House, which has 70 bedrooms. The larger by far is the Resort Hotel, which has 330 rooms, a convention centre with room for 1,500 delegates, and a 13,000 sq ft exhibition hall, which is certainly big enough to be used as the tented village during the Ryder Cup – though it won't be. The tented village will be near the 1st tee of the Ryder Cup course.

It is a matter of some pride to those at Celtic Manor that its three courses offer three different challenges. The Roman Road course, as said, hosted an event on the European Tour and was a stern test for Europe's leading professionals. The Montgomerie course will have a linksy feel to it while those golfers who are brave, good or foolhardy enough to want to try themselves against the ultimate challenge will be able to play the Ryder Cup course.

Just as there are few courses that will offer such good spectator facilities as on the closing holes of the Ryder Cup course, so there are very few venues that offer three different courses.

Early one morning in October 2001 Sir Terry Matthews was heading for Celtic Manor and the site of his birthplace, the Lydia Beynon maternity hospital, when his jet taxied to a halt at Cardiff airport. The first man Matthews saw as he stepped out of his plane stuck out his hand and said: "Well done on the Ryder Cup."

The Mabinogion, that repository of Welsh myths, would have been enhanced if the man who had brought a £100m prize to his home country at a time of economic stress were larger than life, had got off the plane with a cigar in one hand and a magnum of champagne in the other and burst into songs of praise.

That is not Matthews' style. He is a big businessman, a billionaire, but not someone who puts a lot of store by personal aggrandisement. He had heard that Celtic Manor had won golf's biggest prize in a hotel room in Nashville, Tennessee, when he was making a >

Above: The green on the 3rd hole of the Roman Road course may appear wide and inviting but its entrance is narrow.

The 14th hole on the Ryder Cup Course, which here appears so tranquil, will see many exciting moments in September 2010.

"This is not for me, Terry Matthews,"
he said. "This is for Wales... It is a monster
win for Wales... It is uplifting to the spirit of the entire
area. This will affect the national spirit. We can say we
have just won something."

• • • • • • • • • • • • • • • • routine telephone call to his sister back in Wales. Midway through
the conversation Kay Dawes interrupted her brother: "Hang on a
minute, Terry," she said. "They're saying something about the
Ryder Cup on the BBC News. Have a listen." And she put the
telephone next to the television, which might seem to be a Heath
Robinson way of communicating such important news.

At Cardiff airport Matthews adjusted his dark jacket and said
quietly to the man who moments earlier had congratulated him:
"This is not for me, Terry Matthews," he said. "This is for Wales.
The economic spin-off for the country will be enormous,

incalculable. It is a monster win for Wales and Wales needed that sort of win to regain some self-confidence and self-respect. There is a monster steelworks closing down and that is a big setback economically. It is uplifting to the spirit of the entire area. This will affect the national spirit. We can say we have just won something."

BBC Wales TV wanted to interview Matthews on the afternoon of that October day in 2001 and he left the hotel for five minutes to go outside in the rain. As he was wired up he looked across towards the Wentwood Hills course and its proposed new holes and clubhouse for the Ryder Cup. When he came back in he appeared to be bone dry. Clearly the rain was all water off a duck's back to Matthews, the billionaire, the man who had secured the Ryder Cup for Wales. ●

Top: 18th hole on the new Ryder Cup Course.

Above: Terry Matthews, owner of Celtic Manor Resort, had plenty to smile about when he heard that the Ryder Cup was coming to Wales.

Opposite: The Lodge is one of the largest and most luxurious clubhouses in Europe.

Conwy

Coastal golf is always challenging and make no mistake, when the Celtic sea flexes its muscles and the wind blows from the west, the true testing nature of Conwy golf club is revealed.

Conwy Golf Club
18 hole, Par 72 (6,647 yds)
Links course.

If it is true, as Patric Dickinson wrote, that at Aberdovey you should always be prepared to let Bernard Darwin through, something similar could be said about Conwy. John Roger Jones and Clive Brown, perhaps the two most distinguished sons of this club, appear at almost every turn.

Jones, universally known as J.R., a past Wales Amateur champion who represented Wales from 1970 to 1985 and was many times captain of his country, is a member of the Championship Committee of the Royal and Ancient golf club of St Andrews and lives in nearby Rhos-on-Sea. Brown, like J.R. a past Wales Amateur champion and a Wales international from 1970 to 1980, was captain of the Walker Cup team that beat the US at Royal Porthcawl in 1995. Brown is the grandson of Tom Jones, the well-known professional at Maesdu who was the first member of the PGA to be elected a club captain.

It is a place of beauty. Positioned on land known as The Morfa, which is Welsh for the foreland or beach, it is cupped between the Carneddau Mountains, the estuary, and Llandudno's Great Orme.

Not long ago J.R. penned some thoughts about his home club, where he has been a member for more than a half century. This is an extract from what he wrote: "it would be difficult to imagine a better place to play golf than on the links beside the Conwy estuary. On a calm sunny morning at high tide, the main distractions are the flutter of sea birds' wings and the slapping of rope on mast in the estuary. Coastal golf is always challenging

and make no mistake, when the Celtic sea flexes its muscles and the wind blows from the west, the true testing nature of Conwy golf club is revealed. Serious questions are asked of the best ball strikers and rightly so!"

Arrive at Conwy late on a summer's evening and the beauty of the course is evident. It is a links course, though one or two of its last few holes are on land that is not very linksy and unlike the land of the previous 15. There are eucalyptus trees behind the 16th, which are not normally present on a links. There are still some sycamores too, and other non-indigenous trees, though a lot were removed before the final qualifying competition for the Open took place in July 2006. But as the sun begins to sink, and the course steams gently in the heat, you cannot help but be enchanted by the estuary in the distance from which can be heard the slapping of halyards on boat masts and the occasional mewing curlew overhead. It is a place of beauty. Positioned on land known as The Morfa, which is Welsh for the foreland or beach, it is cupped between the Carneddau Mountains, the estuary, and Llandudno's Great Orme. >

Above: Conwy Golf Club from the Vardre, Deganwy, with Conwy Mountain and Anglesey in the distance.

• • • • • • • • • • • • • •

Above: The 2nd green near which were built the Mulberry Harbours used in the D-Day invasion.

Right: It is a long walk up the 5th hole, in the shadow of Conwy Mountain, when played into a stiff prevailing wind.

Funny how often Royal Liverpool golf club and its members feature in a book about golf courses in Wales, isn't it? It was a group of members from Hoylake who first realised the potential of this piece of land and in 1875 arranged for a professionally-designed 12-hole layout. It has also been suggested that visiting Scots had laid out a few holes on which to practise six years before this. The club was officially formed in 1890 and a military mess hut from a neighbouring army camp was used as the first clubhouse. It claims, not very vigorously, that it is the oldest club in Wales, though that honour is more generally accorded to Tenby. In 1895 the course was extended to 18 holes and that same year became one of the founding members of the Welsh Golfing Union.

The course is now 6,647 yards long with a par of 72 and a SSS of 72. Its new clubhouse, with its striking round turrets at each end, was opened by Clive Brown in 1996. The events it has staged make an impressive list and include the Welsh Amateur, the Boys Amateur championship, the British Ladies Open Amateur, the European Boys', the Welsh Amateur Stroke play and the men's and women's Home Internationals. Peter Thomson and Doug

It does not take long before the visitor discovers three of the club's distinctive features, the first being that during the war the Mulberry Harbours used in the D Day landings in northern France were built secretly near what is now the 2nd green...

Sewell, two stroke players if ever there were ones, tied for the Martini International Trophy here in 1970.

It does not take long before the visitor discovers three of the club's distinctive features, the first being that during the war the Mulberry Harbours used in the D-Day landings in northern France were built secretly near what is now the 2nd green but was then the 9th. The second is that almost every hole goes in a direction that is different to its predecessor. I cannot remember a course where this characteristic is so pronounced. As a result >

the wind is an even greater factor at Conwy than at most courses because while there are not two successive holes where the golfer must play into the wind, so there are not two successive holes where the golfer can feel the benefit of it. This partly explains why although its length might seem short by modern yardstick, the course is so difficult. The SSS on the second day of Open qualifying in 2006 was 77. "It was only a light breeze by our standards," notes Duncan Brown, the secretary.

The challenge of Conwy's finish lies in meeting the demand for accuracy that is required from the tees and the approach shots to these three holes.

The last striking feature comprises the three finishing holes, which are of slightly different characteristics. Their difficulty is not caused by length because even from the back tees the 16th, 17th and 18th holes total only a few yards more than 1,100, which is barely two medium length par 5s at many courses.

The challenge of Conwy's finish lies in meeting the demand for accuracy that is required from the tees and the approach shots to these three holes. J.R's best finish is 3,3,3. Frankly if you cover them in level par, that is good going. If even the pros consider them difficult then goodness knows what the average golfer is likely to say about them.

George Duncan was the first club professional, appointed in 1910. Duncan went on to win the Open in 1920, finish second in 1922 yet might be almost as well known for the fact that he beat Walter Hagen in the match between British and US professionals in 1926 and again in the 1929 Ryder Cup. The current professional is Peter Lees, who joined the club in 1966 and was elected President for one year in 2006 as a mark of the members' respect for him.

Above: A summer's evening on the 7th green.

The 9th and 3rd greens
adjoin the Conwy estuary.

Cradoc

...it is now, like an arboretum set down in scenery that can only be described as drop-dead gorgeous.

Cradoc Golf Club
18 hole, Par 71 (6,188 yds)
Parkland course.

Though golf is a highly individual sport, frustrating and very idiosyncratic, it shares one characteristic with other sports that may not be so idiosyncratic or individual. Some of the places where it is played, and some of the places on which it is played for that matter, represent a triumph over odds.

Imagine building a course in the desert, for example, where there is no water to grow grass for the fairways and the greens are oil-based and known as browns as a result. Imagine 70 acres of green belt land in north London, surrounded by houses and with a small reservoir underneath. You wouldn't think that a golf course could be laid out on such a small parcel of land would you, one that almost touched the back gardens of dozens of houses? Well it was and Highgate is a popular and successful club, one nearer the centre of London than any other. Similarly the Dubai Country Club provides golfers with a chance to play an imaginative and different game of golf when they are in the Gulf.

If I said that when considering Cradoc you will discover echoes of both Dubai Country Club and Highgate I mean this to be entirely complimentary.

If I said that when considering Cradoc you will discover echoes of both Dubai Country Club and Highgate I mean this to be entirely complimentary. It is a charming, warm and hospitable golf club set in stunning scenery two miles north-west of Brecon. It isn't far from anywhere but nor is it particularly near anywhere either. One of those who advised at its formation was Bill Graham, the founder of St Pierre, and it was thought some of the principles evident at the Chepstow course could be applied to Penoyre, as it

then was. One difference was immediately obvious. Whereas St Pierre has the M4 within a few miles, Penoyre has no such road system to provide golfers. That is one sense in which it is a triumph over the odds.

Penoyre was begun by a few enthusiasts who felt that the nine-hole course at Brecon that had done such good service was no longer big enough. Furthermore it was on land leased by the Evans family. If you need to be reminded who the Evans family are, then you have not been paying enough attention to Welsh golf. In the centenary history of the Welsh Golfing Union, which I commend, incidentally (and I would because I wrote it), Albert Evans is referred to as the Welsh Daddy. At Portmarnock in 1961 at the age of 51 he not only won his 50th cap for Wales but also captained Wales to their first victory over England in the Home Internationals. The score is worth recounting – 12-3 – and England did not win one singles.

Read the history of Cradoc Golf Club and it quickly becomes obvious that this is a club that had a troubled birth. It began as >

Above: Llangorse Lake, Brecon.

Penoyre Golf Club in the grounds of Penoyre House, which was said to have cost Colonel Lloyd Watkins £100,000 to build and who, perhaps as a result, died penniless. The course was then, as it is now, like an arboretum set down in scenery that can only be described as drop-dead gorgeous.

"No chimney pots, no cars, no traffic, no roads, wild life. This is millionaire's golf at pauper prices."

Bob Barnes, the club manager, was driving a visitor around the course one glorious day in November 2006 when he slowed the buggy to a halt, looked at the views and marvelled. "There's Pen-Y-Fan," he said, pointing at the distinctive Brecon Beacons. "There's Cribbin, and there in the distance are the Black Mountains." He paused for a moment for effect, as if he was drinking in the scenery for the first not the 51st time, before adding: "No chimney pots, no cars, no traffic, no roads...This is millionaires' golf at pauper prices."

Cradoc Golf Club owes a huge amount to a few: to the people who found the land, raised the money, did the necessary deals, badgered the officials and fought tigerishly on behalf of their beloved golf club. Of those who were involved at the beginning John Morrell, an accountant in Brecon, and Les Watkins, a draper in Brecon, are not the only two but they might be two of the most important. There was so much to do and so little time in which to do it. For years the members were not secure. "I think at one point that about 20 members guaranteed £5,000 each to support a bank loan to build the clubhouse that was completed in December 1979," Nick Morrell, son of John, said. "It caused concern among a few wives, I am sure." From the club history one loses count of the number of crises that were averted until, one day, the storm clouds parted, the financial winds that threatened closure, bankruptcy and the like were gone and Cradoc became the club it is today.

I like Brecon and Breconshire and we go back a long time. Somewhere I still have a copy of *Brecon Adventure,* which I read and loved as a child and though it is rather battered now, the >

Above: The old 7th green is no longer in use and has been repositioned. The hole, a par 3, has stunning views over the Brecon Beacons and surrounding countryside.

• • • • • • • • • • • • • • • •

thought of it still brings a smile to my face. My grandparents lived in Brecon, in a street overlooking the old railway station and I remember my grandfather setting off to cycle down to the golf club. Indeed, I remember – I think – the old clubhouse or the pro's shop and in it the lockers of some of the members. I remember the name Marshman seemed to pop up a lot and soon I met Albert Evans, the aforementioned Welsh Daddy, whose family house was on the land of the golf club.

The thing about Cradoc is this.
It has those characteristics that make some of the more remote Irish clubs so welcoming.

The thing about Cradoc is this. It has those characteristics that make some of the more remote Irish clubs so welcoming. They have an abundance of F, A and I. 'F' stands for friendliness, the sort of friendliness that makes a stranger welcome the moment he enters the clubhouse. It might also stand for finance in the sense of value for money because I understand that you can play one round at each of Cradoc, Builth Wells and Llandrindod Wells for £60 and if that is not a bargain then I don't know what is.

'A' stands for atmosphere, which you can create to a certain extent. Leather chairs, a warm fire, a welcoming atmosphere, a beaming barman, all that sort of thing. Cradoc reminds me of the central part in a rural community that a golf club can play and it was no surprise to learn it was named Welsh Golf Club of the Year in 2005.

'I' is for informality. There are no stuffed shirts here. Not many ties either. "We are a very friendly club, a lovely course to play

on," Bob Barnes told me. "There is no waiting list for membership. The club philosophy is to make golf as accessible as possible. We do not put obstacles in the way of members and potential members."

Richard Dixon, the current secretary of the Welsh Golfing Union, remembers helping to clear stones from the greens at Penoyre in 1966/1967 and he was paid £1 for his troubles. It has come a long way since then and so has he.

Richard Dixon, the current secretary of the Welsh Golfing Union, remembers helping to clear stones from the greens at Penoyre in 1966/1967 and he was paid £1 for his troubles. It has come a long way since then and so has he.

Above: The magnificent Brecon Beacons form a backdrop to the 13th green. In the foreground is the tree-clad hill known as The Gaer.

Holyhead

Since the 1950s Holyhead has been its own landlord and master of its own destiny.

Holyhead Golf Club
18 hole, Par 68 (6,090 yds)
Heathland course.

It is not possible to get much farther north-west in Wales than Holyhead on the island of Anglesey. Though it strikes a chord in the minds of many as being the home of the ferry to Dublin and not far from Llanfair PG (of which more later) Holyhead is known among golfers as having a short but testing golf course. It is where David McLean, who represented Wales from 1968 until 1990, has played all his life and where the British Girls Championship was held in 1998.

So many golf courses in Wales have links with railways it comes as no surprise to discover that Holyhead is another.

So many golf courses in Wales have links with railways it comes as no surprise to discover that Holyhead is another. The way in which Harlech, Aberdovey and Tenby were nourished by the regular supply of visitors borne there aboard trains is well chronicled. Less so is the part the old London, Midland and Scotland Railway played in establishing Holyhead as a golfing destination. The reasoning is the same, though.

The LMS brought passengers to Holyhead on trains that were also carrying post that would be unloaded onto and collected from the mail boats that travelled to and from Ireland. LMS wanted something for the passengers to do while waiting for trains and golf seemed the obvious thing. The Railway Hotel was a splendid place to stay; Holyhead golf club, laid out by James Braid in 1912, became a splendid place to play and taxis ferried them between the two. For hotel residents, golf was free.

An article in an Anglesey paper recounts how 70 players teed off at the opening of the course on 3 August 1914. Ten days later only

The chimney at the Anglesey Aluminium factory is a ready landmark from many points of the course.

10 members could get to the 1st tee. The reason? It was the day that the first World War broke out.

The chimney at the Anglesey Aluminium factory is a ready landmark from numerous points of the course. It seems to be in the background wherever you look. Anglesey Aluminium, RAF Valley, the docks, Wylfa power station are all the sorts of employment opportunities that brought people to Anglesey – after which they often joined the golf club. In 1950 the LMS sold the land to the members in the form of debentures totalling £12,000 and since then the club has been its own landlord and master of its own destiny.

These days you need to be careful where you're going lest you unwittingly get in the way of players on another hole. The 6th seems to cross the 7th, the 8th and 9th run side by side in opposite directions, the 14th and 18th tees adjoin one another. >

Above: Brunel's suspension bridge over the Menai Straits is the gateway to Anglesey.

It is when you reach the higher ground of the 10th, a par 5 that runs to the farthest point of the course from the clubhouse, that you get a sense of space. On the 11th tee you can be sure of staying dry and probably warm no matter which direction the wind is blowing because there is a four-sided, sturdy wooden structure in which to shelter. Into the wind the 18th is a difficult hole on which to get a par.

"It started out as a nine-hole course but quickly became 18 holes," Barbara Jones, who probably knows more about the club

These days you need to be careful where you're going lest you unwittingly get in the way of players on another hole. The 6th seems to cross the 7th, the 8th and 9th run side by side in opposite directions, the 14th and 18th tees adjoin one another.

than any other living person, explained. "Braid's design was based on Scottish golf courses. It is heathland and its main problem is gorse. Though it is on 104 acres there is no space for it to expand, so by modern standards it is not long but you have to be straight. The gorse bushes are real ball gobblers.

"My claim to fame lies in the fact that my maternal grandfather, George Frederick Bullock, came here as the pro from Robin Hood golf club near Solihull in 1929 and my mother and two brothers, also George Frederick and Jimmy (who both became pros) were brought up in the cottage at the side of the 9th fairway. It has fallen into disrepair now and the garden sheds are used as a place for the greenkeeping staff to keep their vehicles.

"Uncle George (or Fred, as he was known in golfing circles) was runner-up in the Open in 1959, when Gary Player won his first Open, so I have been associated with the club most of my life.

"Uncle Fred is still alive but he suffers from motor neurone disease and lives in a home in Hendon. It so happens that the >

Above: Best be accurate here. The 5th green and 6th tee are very close to one another.

day of his 70th birthday was the day of a fund-raising competition for Motor Neurone Disease Association at a nearby golf club and Peter Alliss and Terry Wogan arranged for him to be taken around the course in a buggy. That was kind of them.

"Uncle Fred is still alive but he suffers from motor neurone disease and lives in a home in Hendon...Peter Alliss and Terry Wogan arranged for him to be taken around the course in a buggy. That was kind of them.

"Uncle Fred was leading the Open at Muirfield by three strokes on the last day when his ball became plugged in a bunker and he took three to get out. That allowed Gary Player to overtake him and win. Uncle Fred tied with Flory van Donck for second, two strokes behind Gary Player. That is the way we talked about it in the family at any rate."

Uncle Fred tied with Flory van Donck for second, two strokes behind Gary Player. That is the way we talked about it in the family at any rate."

And Llanfair PG? Ah, yes. You will be glad you asked. Having crossed the Menai Straits you cannot travel very far on Anglesey without coming across the village with the hugely long name. Llanfair PG is its abbreviated name, the name by which it is known but its full name is Llanfairpwllgwyngyllgogerych-wyrndrobwllllantysiliogogogoch and this appears on signs at the railway station. It means, roughly speaking, Saint Ysilio and Mary at a church in a hollow close to a white hazel which is near a whirlpool and a red cave. Or something like that.

Left: The views out to sea, as shown from the 2nd green stand comparison with any.

Below: You don't often see rocky outcrops like these on the 7th on courses adjoining the sea.

Ascending a staircase to heaven. Climbing the undulating fairway of the 18th green.

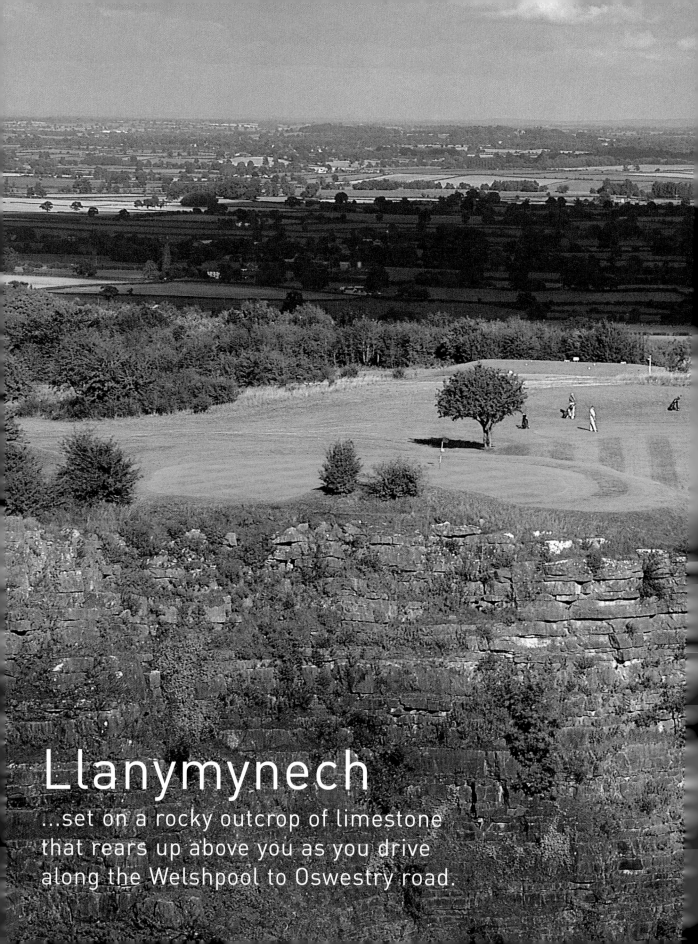

Llanymynech

...set on a rocky outcrop of limestone
that rears up above you as you drive
along the Welshpool to Oswestry road.

Llanymynech Golf Club
18 hole, Par 70 (6,047 yds)
Mountain course.

"I know who'll tell me all about Llanymynech," I thought to myself before setting out to drive to Oswestry. "Dai Davies will know. I'll give him a call." Before he joined *The Guardian* in the mid 1980s, Davies worked for the *Birmingham Post* for years and not much happened in golf in the Midlands without him knowing about it and if it did then someone would have to answer to him. He did not travel to many tournaments abroad but if a golfer from his parish did well he was on the telephone in an instant.

"For me the thing about Llanymynech is that on one hole you tee off in Wales and drive into England" Bob Davies said.

Dai, however, was not at home when I telephoned him but was tending his vineyard in Australia, as one does. So I tried Bob Davies, another colleague. Bob Davies is a substantial figure in the Midlands in more ways than one, having been the secretary of the Shropshire and Herefordshire County Unions for the past 29 years as well as past captain and President of Shrewsbury Golf Club at Condover. For more than 30 years, until his retirement in 2002, he was the golf writer for either the *Shropshire Star* or the *Wolverhampton Express and Star*.

"For me the thing about Llanymynech is that on one hole you tee off in Wales and drive into England," Bob Davies said. "One of its attractions is its height and therefore, the views. It was where Ian Woosnam started playing golf. He was a very keen footballer and very good too but Harold, his father, thought Ian was too small and would get injured so he made him turn to golf. Bernard Thomas, the junior organiser in those days, was very strict. He organised the kids on a Saturday morning and made sure they

always started on the putting green before they were allowed out on to the course.

"Llanymynech has produced a lot of good golfers," Davies continued. "Philip Parkin played there for a while when he wanted to represent Shropshire. Mark Trow, who has played for Wales as a boy and a senior international, is currently on a golf scholarship to the US. Andy Griffiths was a direct contemporary of Ian Woosnam's, turned pro and competed in two Opens and played the European Tour before returning to Llanymynech to become the club's professional. Basil Griffiths, his brother, is one of Wales's best seniors."

As well as having a name that anyone not born in Wales finds almost unpronounceable, Llanymynech is unusual in that two of its first three holes are short holes and it has five par 3s and three par 5s in all. It is also unusual, as Bob Davies has recounted, in that on the 4th you drive from Wales and putt out in England. In fact it has 15 holes in Wales and three in England. >

Above: Powis Castle, Welshpool.

• • • • • • • • • • • • • • • •   There are courses that straddle roads and counties but not many that straddle countries. On land that adjoins the course are lead mines, lime kilns and caves. It is an historical treasure trove and as such closely protected by the Heritage experts. On a bank behind the 6th green is a plaque pointing out that the bank was part of Offa's Dyke, which divided Wales from England, and on this site in AD 51 Caradoc (also known as Caractacus) made his last stand against the Romans.

On a bank behind the 6th green is a plaque pointing out that the bank was part of Offa's Dyke, which divided Wales from England.

Many golf courses in Wales have stunning views. Nefyn, Harlech, Aberdovey, Conwy, Holyhead, Royal Porthcawl, Cradoc and of these Cradoc might have the best. But good as they are, they do not compare with views at Llanymynech which is set on a rocky outcrop of limestone that rears up above you as you drive along the Welshpool to Oswestry road. From the 12th tee the views are simply staggering. "This is our front garden," Howard Jones, the club secretary said, pointing out a vista that included Shropshire, Staffordshire, Cheshire. Then he turned round and gesticulated towards north Wales and the rumpled hills in the distance. "And this is our back garden." Do a full 360 degree sweep from the 12th tee and it is possible to see seven of the old shire counties – Flintshire, Denbighshire, Montgomeryshire, Merionethshire, Staffordshire, Cheshire and Shropshire.

The day I made my most recent visit to Llanymynech, a few members were present to help me with my research. I met Stuart

Penrose, who would shortly become an assistant pro at the club,
Neville Kynaston and Ken Evans as well as Andy Griffiths.
Neville Kynaston came in with about 20 sheets of yellow paper.
One side contained a list of items for sale at Oswestry Electrical
& Plumbing Factory, the other, in his neat, printed handwriting,
an account of the early years of the club.

"Llanymynech, affectionately known as The Hill, has been in
circulation since 1933," he wrote. "Prior to that date part of the
course was the original Oswestry Golf Club. The Oswestry Golf
Club was reformed at Aston Park in 1931."

There followed a list of the trials and tribulations, triumphs and
disasters with which many golf clubs would be familiar: sheep
grazing the course in the 30s; Mrs Rose Griffiths taking over the
catering of teas on Saturdays and Sundays and being allowed to
purchase two Primus stoves for this purpose; collecting water
for use in the locker room in a butt off the clubhouse roof;
mains elecricity and mains water arriving at the club in 1960.
And so on. >

Above: Holing out on the
18th green.

Approach to 13th green with
Berwyn Mountains in the
distance.

Ian Woosnam

My colleague Scott Michaux, the golf writer of *The Augusta Chronicle* in Georgia, visited Llanymynech in mid-summer 2006 on his way to the Open to gather the material for a feature he was writing about Woosnam, one that would appear at the time of the Ryder Cup. He told me later how puzzled he was that so little was made of Europe's Ryder Cup captain at the club.

From the 12th tee the views are simply staggering. "This is our front garden" Howard Jones, the club secretary said, pointing out a vista that included Shropshire, Staffordshire, Cheshire.

In fact, a lot is made of the Woosnam name, not quite so much of Ian. Harold, his father, who died in 2003, was captain in 1973 two years after Joan Woosnam, Ian's mother, was lady captain. Harold and Chris Kynaston, Neville's brother, won the Arthur Prince Cup in 1964. Ian is up on one of the club's honours boards for having won a foursomes competition with his mother in 1976 – the Family Cup. There are photographs of him as a boy. Howard Jones pointed out that the club was going to have a Woosnam wall too.

To say the club is proud of Ian Woosnam would be an understatement yet Michaux noted mischievously what was said on the club's website. "A group of former clubmates and county player colleagues spent days pleading with him [Ian Woosnam] not to take such a drastic step [as turning professional] because they reckoned he was no better than thousands of other single player amateurs, including themselves, and one day would come to regret the foolish decision."

As clubhouses go, even Llanymynech's most ardent supporter would not say theirs is a thing of beauty, an architectural gem. The point about a clubhouse is that it is not the exterior that matters so much as the interior. It's like a watch. You want it to look all right on your wrist but it is much more important that all the gears mesh.

The clubhouse is a talking point, adding to the popularity of the club, which is considerable judging by the letters on the club's website. Most were of the "I came, I saw and I fell in love" variety. One, though, was slightly different. It read: "Wednesday, played the course; Thursday, downloaded membership application form; Friday, joined. Is this a record?" If it's not, then I would like to hear who has done better than that! ●

Above: Seven counties are visible from the 12th tee, four in Wales and three in England.

Machynys

The course is in two distinct loops, the outward
one being the more parkland like, the inward
one having a nodding acquaintance with the sea.

Macynys Golf Club
18 hole, Par 72 (7,051 yds)
Links course.

The first time I saw Machynys, I couldn't see it. Nor could anyone else. It was breakfast time on a September morning in 2003 and a group of us including Jim Anderson, the developer, and Gary Nicklaus, who had been involved with the design team assembled by Jack, his father, had gathered to see the progress that was being made on the first Nicklaus course in Wales. Unfortunately fog kept visibility to 100 yards or so, if that.

For one thing it is in a beautiful position, adjoining the Wild Fowl and Wetlands Trust at Penclacwydd to the east and overlooking Carmarthen Bay, then rimmed by the adjoining Millennium Coastal Park...

Soon though, the course was opened with a fanfare, quickly making a name for itself and being voted the best new course in Britain in 2005 by two golf magazines as well as the host venue for the 2005 and 2006 Wales Ladies Championship of Europe as part of the build-up to the 2010 Ryder Cup at Celtic Manor. One glorious summer's day I pointed the car west for Carmarthenshire, the county of my birth. It did not take me long to realise that while Llanelli needs a bit of imagination to be described as beautiful, though the rugby the Scarlets play can sometimes be so described, there need be no such reluctance when it comes to Machynys. For one thing it is in a beautiful position, adjoining the Wild Fowl and Wetlands Trust at Penclacwydd to the east and overlooking Carmarthen Bay, then rimmed by the adjoining Millennium Coastal Park which features a 22-km uninterrupted coastal path from the Loughor bridge to Pembrey Country Park. Even some of Machynys's inland holes

have a kind of majesty as they sweep up to and away from the Trostre Tinplate Works, the town's sole remaining link with the tinplate trade.

Machynys has 18 miles of piping in all and a whopping 25 acres of both salt and fresh water for lakes.

Want to know how much it cost to build a modern golf complex with a Nicklaus Design course? It might be vulgar to talk about money but in this context it is instructive. Three million pounds, four million, five million? Remember how much water there always is on Nicklaus courses in the form of lakes and ponds. Think of the irrigation and drainage piping that is needed. Machynys has 18 miles of piping in all and a whopping 25 acres of both salt and fresh water for lakes. Think of the differing grasses needing to be sown, the amount of earth removed, the mounding, the building of the greens. Think of the requirements of a modern clubhouse, a gym and spa, a restaurant, a pro's shop, a teaching centre. Remember all these and you begin to understand why it >

Above: A wild fowl sanctuary adjoins the course.

• • • • • • • • • • • • • • • •

cost £7.5m: £3.5m for the course and £4m for a spanking new, up-to-the-minute clubhouse. And to think that once golf clubs were little more than a locker room, a bar and a golf course.

You climb circular stairs to a wrap-around restaurant, public area, bar which shows off Carmarthen Bay and the golf course to their fullest glory...

Above: A spectacular sunset seen from the clubhouse looking over the back nine.

Right: A fast downhill putt on the 13th hole.

Opposite: Canada Geese have made their home on a pond near the 11th green.

The clubhouse is a good example of modern golf club architecture. In recent years the trend has been to put the working areas such as the locker rooms and lavatories, which do not need views, on the ground floors and the public areas upstairs to give an outward-looking aspect. The Irish started it when they built new clubhouses at clubs such as Killarney and Tralee, where the views are spectacular, and at Machynys this has been embraced fully. The large and extensive gym is on the ground floor, just past the pro's shop. It has 35 stations, a Jacuzzi, six beauty treatment and massage rooms, a steam room, a sauna and a specialist aromatherapy room. You climb circular

stairs to a wrap-around restaurant, public area, bar which shows off Carmarthen Bay and the golf course to their fullest glory and almost a 360-degree view. The bar is run by the people from Fairyhill – the outstanding restaurant at Reynoldston on the Gower across the water. It can seat 80. There are also two lounges, a large sundeck and conference facilities for up to 100.

The course is in two distinct loops, the outward one being the more parkland-like, the inward one having a nodding acquaintance with the sea. As you drive away and look at the practice ground on your right, it has a parkland feeling to it. The long 13th hole has hints of a parkland course about it, as do the 10th and the short 11th where the honking Canada geese landing and taking off from the nearby pond seem intent on making such a mess. A suggestion: move the pond or move the green. And then you walk past the development of houses and head towards the water and the 14th hole that curves gently along the shore and suddenly, it looks like a links course once more – and smells like one too. >

In a brilliant essay about linksland in *Golf International*, David Purdie explained how encouraging wildlife on the ground attracts a variety of birds above it. Kill off the life on the ground and you get no activity up above, he wrote. The most vocal skylarks I have ever known are at Royal St George's in Sandwich where the course takes up 150 acres of a 350-acre site and the 200 acres that are not used are covered in marram grass. Voles, moles, rats, field mice and many other animals are able to run riot on the ground and the skylarks seem to celebrate the continued supply of food with their tuneful noises up above. There is birdsong at times at Machynys too and attempts have been made to attract water voles and to provide halts for otters by making the lakes shallow sided so that animals can get in and out of them.

Gary Nicklaus, who oversaw the project design on behalf of his father, has identified the 411-yard 4th, the 392-yard 5th, the 451-yard 16th, and the 516-yard 18th as some of his favourite and most challenging holes. "The 4th is the most unique, a short-ish

par 4 but a very challenging and a difficult one nonetheless," Gary said. "The 16th, a par 4 that is played across the lake from right behind the clubhouse, is probably one of the most beautiful holes on the course. The view from the green of the whole bay is spectacular, whether the tide is in or out." I agree but then I would. I nearly birdied it the last time I played it.

Jim Anderson, who developed Hanbury Manor in Hertfordshire, is the key man behind Machynys. He persuaded the Nicklaus organisation to join him and his partners in the autumn of 1999 in what was then known as the Nicklaus Joint Venture Group. When Anderson made his first visit to Carmarthenshire it was the first time he had crossed the Severn Bridge. "When we saw the land we thought we could do something pretty special here," Anderson recalled during the 2006 Wales Ladies Championship of Europe. Suffice to say they have. ●

Above: "We were blown away by its splendor" – Golf World 2005. The 15th green and beyond under snow.

Above: This is what the 15th green looks like in warmer conditions.

Nefyn

One of Nefyn's boasts is the same as one of Royal Porthcawl's, namely that you can see the sea from every tee on the course.

Nefyn & District Golf Club
The Links courses consist of a
front 10 holes and two distinctly
different back 8 holes.
Old Course – 18 hole, Par 70/71
(6,138 yds) New Course –
18 hole, Par 71 (6,548 yds).

Everyone has a golf course they regard with greater affection than any other. Bernard Darwin's was Aberdovey. "Not that I make for it any claim that it is the best, not even on the strength of its alphabetical pre-eminence but because it is the course that my soul loves best of all the courses in the world," Darwin wrote.

Darwin's Aberdovey is my Nefyn...

Darwin's Aberdovey is my Nefyn, which is on the Lleyn peninsula a couple of hours' drive north of Aberdovey. I first played there about 50 years ago when we spent family holidays in the Nefyn and Morfa Nefyn area and even all these years later I have been left with the clearest, most wonderful memories.

For a few glorious weeks each summer we enjoyed a Swallows and Amazons existence, sort of. We rented Dros-Y-Mor, a house on stilts on the little bay the Nefyn side of Porthdinllaen. A cliff path led down to it from the old 10th hole on the peninsula nine. At night my brother and I would walk up to the Bay Tree, a coffee bar in Morfa Nefyn, to meet our friends. We could have gone to the Tŷ Coch pub in Porthdinllaen, which was much closer, except that we were not old enough.

I went into the Tŷ Coch for the first time on a blazing hot day in 2006. It was thriving and the proprietor, who was behind the bar, told me proudly: "I've been here all my life. And I never want to go anywhere else. I was born here, the first person born on the beach in 110 years. I made news that day and I've been doing so ever since."

By day, all those years ago, we sailed around the coast using a borrowed motor boat to catch mackerel that we would bring back

Opposite: The Tŷ Coch pub at Porthdinllaen is below the 15th and a possible destination for either a stray drive or a thirsty golfer.

for my mother to cook. At least my brother and the rest of my family did. I was on the golf course most of the time, climbing the zig-zag cliff path in the mornings and returning, downhill and downwind, at lunchtime.

I played with a number of juniors of the same age, two of whom were particularly gifted. Paul Smart still lives in the area, still >

I went into the Tŷ Coch for the first time on a blazing hot day in 2006. It was thriving and the proprietor, who was behind the bar, told me proudly: "I've been here all my life. And I never want to go anywhere else. I was born here, the first person born on the beach in 110 years. I made news that day and I've been doing so ever since."

• • • • • • • • • • • • • • • •

plays golf well. The other was David Parsonage, the son of the coastguard. A very talented golfer with a picture book swing, he led the Carris Boys' Trophy at the halfway point one year. He was always going to turn professional and he duly did so and was for a time assistant to Eamonn Darcy at Erewash Valley golf club in Derbyshire. Sadly he committed suicide there.

One of Nefyn's boasts is the same as one of Royal Porthcawl's, namely that you can see the sea from every tee on the course. For all that, though, I remain more struck by the fact that so many of the holes hug the coastline. How often have I stood on the back tee of the 2nd, perhaps 370 yards from the green with a strong wind in my face and the sea gurgling noisily to the right, and thought: "it's going to take three bloody good shots to get on in two from here"?

Nefyn is known for the views from the course, across to Anglesey, to Snowdonia, to the Wicklow Mountains in Ireland. I remember it more for the quality of its tees, which are often raised, often surrounded by soft, springy turf and all presenting challenging

Above: Take your pick as a backdrop to your golf, the sea or the beach.

Right: A lapse in concentration on the 13th green could be forgiven, situated as it is between rocky outcrops and the water's edge, with the north Wales coastline and maybe a dolphin or seal in the background.

tee shots. What is more difficult than the drive from the 13th on the peninsula nine? You take off as much of the carry across the cliffs as you dare. Play it on a day when the wind is coming from the right and it is as difficult a drive as any in Wales.

On the new 5th tee on windy days spume lands on you, thrown up by the sea crashing on rocks behind and below you. I always got a kick from climbing on to the 17th on the peninsula nine and, for that matter, up to the old 15th with Anglesey in the background and Lifeboat Bay to the left. I still hold in my head a smell of >

How often have I stood on the back tee of the 2nd, perhaps 370 yards from the green with a strong wind in my face and the sea gurgling noisily to the right, and thought: "it's going to take three bloody good shots to get on in two from here?"

the grass surrounding these tees. I wish I could say I approve of the tee of the old 14th, which is now built on a concrete tower ten feet above the ground. You hit from an artificial surface and it feels like playing from a ski jump. My favourite watching place in all golf is to the left of the 12th at Royal Birkdale, high up on the side of a sand dune nestling in grass that is as comfortable as a plumped-up eiderdown. But the green of the 13th on the peninsula nine at Nefyn runs it close. It sits between rocky outcrops of moss-covered rock, cradled as if in a man's hand. The sea is beyond, the rocks to either side.

...the late George Houghton, the writer, reported the secretary of Nefyn as describing the peninsula nine holes as "like playing on the deck of an aircraft carrier". That was an apt description.

I always felt twin emotions when we clattered past the clubhouse round to the old 10th on the peninsula nine: excited at what I was about to see and nervous that I would hit a shot or two over a cliff. In his book *Golf Addict invades Wales*, the late George Houghton reported the secretary of Nefyn as describing the peninsula nine holes as "like playing on the deck of an aircraft carrier". That was an apt portrayal.

If Harlech is much as I remember it from the 1960s, Nefyn has not altered that much either. I could still find my way into and around the clubhouse, though the upstairs room where juniors were able to pass the time when they were not on the golf course, which was not often, is almost certainly used for other things. Even if I were blindfolded I would back myself to know my way to the pro's shop. I used to spend hours in there when it was raining listening to Dennis Grace telling stories and wishing that the rain would stop so that I could get out and play golf again.

Fifty years ago as a small boy I would sit in The Pot, the blowhole over which you hit your shot on the short 16th. As balls thudded into the grass I would make a mental note of where they had landed. "Seen my ball?" I was asked many times. "No, sorry," I replied, flashing a butter-wouldn't-melt-in-my-mouth smile. That was how I kept myself in balls 50 years ago.

By coincidence last summer I watched a men's fourball tee off on the same hole and saw one ball plunge into the blowhole. Momentarily I was transported back to my childhood. I ran over to try to mark the ball. This time I thought I would repay my debt to society by finding the missing ball and returning it to its owner. So much for my good intentions. It was nowhere to be seen.

Tenby is sporty, a reminder of what golf was like 110 years ago; Harlech is difficult; Royal Porthcawl is scenic. Nefyn is sporty, too, difficult on a windy day, and, above all else, plain good fun; a course where the vicissitudes of sloping lies and shared fairways just don't seem to matter as much as they do elsewhere. It has remained the course I love above all others for the past 50 years and there is no chance of it losing its place in my heart in the next half century.

The 15th tee requires a
long accurate carry over
the cliff-edge to the fairway
and blinkers to block out
the distractions of the
surrounding panorama.

Pyle & Kenfig

"The front nine is sturdy, typical downland or moorland turf and played from the back tees on a windy day would present a considerable test. But the run of holes from the 11th to the 16th are sensational."

Pyle & Kenfig Golf Club
18 hole, Par 71 (6,588 yds)
Heathland/Links course.

If memory serves, is what they say, isn't it? Well on this occasion it doesn't. For the life of me I cannot remember whether I played Pyle and Kenfig when I was a boy or, indeed, whether I had ever been there before I visited the week of the 2006 Welsh Amateur Championship? I rather think not because I got lost in the Bermuda Triangle of North and South Cornelly, the Kenfig industrial estate and the water works.

The back nine to the west is, well, just mouth-watering, passing through duneland, going close to Sker Farm and the ruins of Sker House that RD Blackmore made famous in his novel "The Maid of Sker."

But it was worth getting lost. After I came off the course my senses were reeling, and, windblown and excited, I raced up the stairs to the office of David Fellowes, the club secretary. The words "Well, what did you think? Was it how you remembered it?" were hardly out of his mouth when I launched into what can only be described as a paean of praise. "I have just seen one of the finest eight holes imaginable," I said. "The front nine is sturdy, typical downland or moorland turf and played from the back tees on a windy day would present a considerable test. But the run of holes from the 11th to the 16th is sensational."

"So you didn't like it then," Fellowes remarked drily. >

Opposite: Sker House, made famous by R.D. Blackmore in his novel The Maid of Sker, ovelooks the dog legged 13th fairway.

Mackenzie Ross, the eminent course architect, had a hand in the
making of P & K as we know it today. The man who designed the
Ailsa course at Turnberry redesigned P & K's inward nine holes
just after the Second World War and he was paid £72 15s 8d for
doing so. "It is noted that golfers at times did not seize upon flat
pasture for their golf courses," Ross wrote in the late 1940s. At
P & K they certainly did not choose flat pasture. They chose land
that was divided by a road and it could scarcely be land that is
more different if the road were 100 miles wide. The front nine, to
the east, displays the character of downland or moorland and is
on higher ground. The back nine to the west is, well, just mouth-
watering, passing through duneland, going close to Sker Farm
and the ruins of Sker House that R.D. Blackmore made famous in
his novel *The Maid of Sker*.

When holes run through dunes as they do at Waterville in Ireland,
say, or Royal Birkdale in England, they can sometimes, not
always but sometimes, have quite narrow fairways because there
is little flat ground between said dunes. That simply isn't the case
at P & K, which is on a hog's back for space on the inward nine

holes. At P & K they are like Royal St George's in Sandwich in Kent, where one course is laid out over 350 acres and there is room for at least one more within the same land.

Moving slowly around P & K's back nine in a buggy, I was not always aware of precisely where to point the wheels because there seemed to be so many paths lined by ferns and gorse bushes. Ferns and P & K are interwoven. In the late 1940s and early 1950s labourers were hired annually to scythe away the ferns and these days they remain an essential part of the course's defences.

Starting at the turning point of the 11th fairway, I noticed with pleasure how the green was snuggling down between two tawny-coloured shoulders of dune and how vividly the red flag stood out against the brown and green background. The only par 5 on the second nine, it looked formidably challenging. The same applied to the 12th, a long par 3. It looked visually pleasing from the tee and there was no sense of going along a corridor through towering, or otherwise, dunes. >

Above: The 11th is a demanding par 5 that has a bunkered narrow entrance to the green.

Then it changed again. To get to the back tee of the 13th you climb up to a tee perhaps 25 feet above the green. There is farmland in the distance to the left and a sea of dunes and ferns to the right. There is no obvious landing area for your drive and if you can't carry the ball 200 or so yards you will find it a very difficult hole. You simply have to take your courage in both hands and aim at the marker post. Having walked along a path lined with more gorse bushes and ferns you reach a clearing where the fairway turns to the right and the flag is visible in the distance.

There is no obvious landing area for your drive and if you can't carry the ball 200 or so yards you will find it a very difficult hole.

The 14th requires another blind drive. Behind the tee are acres of sand dune and from this tee you can hear the rumble and hiss of the sea. It is the land out beyond this hole upon which the club is hoping one day to be able to make some new holes. Plans were made some years ago for just such an extension but financial considerations and environmental fears meant no further progress was made.

As if there hasn't been enough of a test already, now comes a testing finish comprising a long par 3 and three par 4s that total nearly 1,500 yards. The 15th, the par 3, is to a green in a dell from where it is impossible to see a house or any sign of life in any direction. On this green you could be in a world of your own. The 16th is a straight hole at last and in the distance can be glimpsed the houses to the left of the 6th. The 17th is another straight one, the longest and perhaps the most difficult of the closing stretch.

Though the truly heroic holes are behind you, one last test remains and that is to clear the ferns and gorse in front of the 18th tee. It is possible to see where you are going only from the metal tower adjacent to the back tee. Once on the fairway a sense of order returns, leading as it does to a flat green 436 yards away.

In 2006 Pyle & Kenfig staged the Welsh Amateur in July and August and a very short time later the men's Home Internationals for the first time. As I drove home I found my mind was dominated by two thoughts. The first was of the remarkable 61, ten under par, by Richard Finch in the pre-qualifying for the 2000 Amateur Championship at Royal Porthcawl. Finch had beaten the previous record by seven strokes. I marvelled at that score and as I did so I smiled to myself at the thought that after the Home Internationals a number of very good amateur golfers from England, Scotland and Ireland would become as enchanted with P & K as I had been. ●

Above: Scenically attractive but difficult to play – the 15th, the last par 3, is well guarded by bunkers.

The land beyond the 14th hole in the background here is where the club hopes to build some new holes.

Royal Porthcawl

...a noble links that has stood the test of time.

Royal Porthcawl Golf Club
18 hole, Par 72 (6,829 yds)
Links course.

There is so much more to the experience of golf at a particular course than just teeing off at the 1st and holing out on the 18th. More than almost any other club, Royal Porthcawl demonstrates just how much more. Its members would say it is the best club in Wales, which is a point to be contested no doubt by Royal St David's, Harlech. But what is indubitably true about Porthcawl is that it has one of the most atmospheric clubhouses in golf, one of the largest and most expansive practice grounds and a noble links that has stood the test of time.

Even the rest home to the right of the clubhouse, where Florence Nightingale once helped out and which is so often mistaken for the clubhouse, adds to the dignity of the drive in to the golf club.

This is not the end of the charms of Royal Porthcawl. Just as some of the considerable attraction of village cricket lies in the appeal of a game on the village green with perhaps a church and a pub in the background, so the approach to a golf club can heighten the excitement of the whole golfing experience. One thinks, for example, of the moment you leave the road to get to Royal Birkdale and turn towards the clubhouse and see the regal dunes topped with waving marram grass. One thinks also of the road over the marshes that guards the entrance to Royal West Norfolk, which for maximum effect must be driven over when the mist is just rising and birds are crying mournfully overhead.

Arriving at Royal Porthcawl the visitor circumnavigates a few roundabouts, passes quickly through a housing estate that no one would call beguiling and then, suddenly, it is there ahead of you.

In the foreground is Lock's Common with its brilliantly green, spongy turf. It was here that the original holes of the RPGC were laid out and remained that way until cattle, camping and carriage wheels combined to become too much of a nuisance.

In the distance one might be able to see one of John Masefield's smoke-stacked steamers battling its way down the Bristol Channel.

In the distance one might be able to see one of John Masefield's smoke-stacked steamers battling its way down the Bristol Channel. John Jermine, who won the Wales Amateur Championship when he was 54, once said that no matter how far he had driven and how tired he was, his spirits were lifted by the first sight of Porthcawl's clubhouse nestling down near the sea and the thought of the course beyond. Even the rest home to the right of the clubhouse, where Florence Nightingale once helped out and which is so often mistaken for the clubhouse, adds to the dignity of the drive in to the golf club. >

Above: Looking back from the 18th green towards the Secretary's office with the Rest Home in the background. The picture gives no sense of the slopes on the green where many golfers have taken three putts – at least.

Since the last years of the 19th century golfers have sought the sanctuary of golf at Royal Porthcawl. For well over one century they have hung their jackets on hooks that look as though they are over one hundred years old, sat on benches that have served thousands of golfers down the years and noted the memorabilia that surrounds them – the photographs of the club captains for example, the portrait of Edward VIII, the Prince of Wales, who would become a patron of the club. The portrait bears closer scrutiny. Wearing a jacket with the top two of the three buttons done up and with an upended club in his left hand, the future Edward VIII looks every inch the golfing charmer. HRH played there in December 1932 on a day when it was so windy that a coastguard had to climb up a very wobbly pole to secure the club flag. The Prince arrived the night before on board the Royal train and slept the night in a siding.

The visitors may pass through two bars, known as Trap One and Trap Two, and then out of the clubhouse, past the pro's shop, the secretary's office and up to the 1st tee where they will confront a magnificent course that has the true characteristics of a links

Above: The red beach hut, now just a landmark, is seen in the background of the 1st green. It was originally by the old first tee, but now is sadly out of play due to health and safety issues.

course and, in addition, the bonus of having the sea being visible from every hole. Its first three holes run parallel with the shore before the course turns inland and twists and winds over terrain that could be described as uplands, containing waving banks of broom and gorse and some heather, not always what you expect on a links.

Its first three holes run parallel with the shore before the course turns inland and twists and winds over terrain that could be described as uplands...

By the 18th, the hallmarks of a links course have reappeared and from the tee the hole slopes gently down towards the sea. Sometimes the sun is setting, casting a glassy sheen over the green. One of the most pleasant places to spend time on a summer's afternoon is on a bench in the lee of the clubhouse, looking across the Channel to the long dark line of the Somerset coast. >

Above: The short 4th hole has a fiercely sloping green and requires a precise tee shot. Come up short and your ball will roll back to the bottom of the green. Be pleased with a par.

If it is a feature of Porthcawl that you can see the sea from every hole, then it is also a feature of the course that it is rarely played without a wind. One winter's night in 1990 the wind was so strong it blew the professional's shop away, the splintered remains being found in the car park the next morning. An odd local climatic conundrum renders the course more benign than might be expected, for often, as local lore has it, storms blowing across from the south-west England divide when they hit the foreshore, one section heading east to Cardiff and one west to Swansea.

If it is a feature of Porthcawl that you can see the sea from every hole, then it is also a feature of the course that it is rarely played without a wind.

It is said that you can tell the quality of a man's reading by the books on his shelf. By that yardstick then the quality of a golf course can be measured by the standard of the champions who have prevailed over it and the championships it has staged. Peter Thomson, the Australian, won the Dunlop Masters by eight

One winter's night in 1990 the wind was so strong it blew the professional's shop away.

strokes here. Dick Chapman, at the time the finest amateur in the world, came from the US to defeat Charlie Coe in the final of the 1951 Amateur, Coe beating Albert Evans, a great figure in golf in Wales, in a semi-final. In 1980 Duncan Evans became the first Welshman to win the Amateur on Welsh soil – at Royal Porthcawl. Perhaps the best-known name who was not a professional was that of Michael Bonallack, who won the Amateur here in 1965. No one could stop the man, who would in due course become the secretary of the Royal and Ancient Golf Club of St Andrews, from winning his second Amateur, not even Clive Clark, who was six up after 13 holes of the 36-hole final.

Below: The 1st appears to be a deceptively easy starting hole, but find the bunkers and a six can be on the card. At Royal Porthcawl, more than most, you must avoid the bunkers to stand a chance of mastering the course.

The 2nd hole is among the toughest on the course. Beware of the beach.

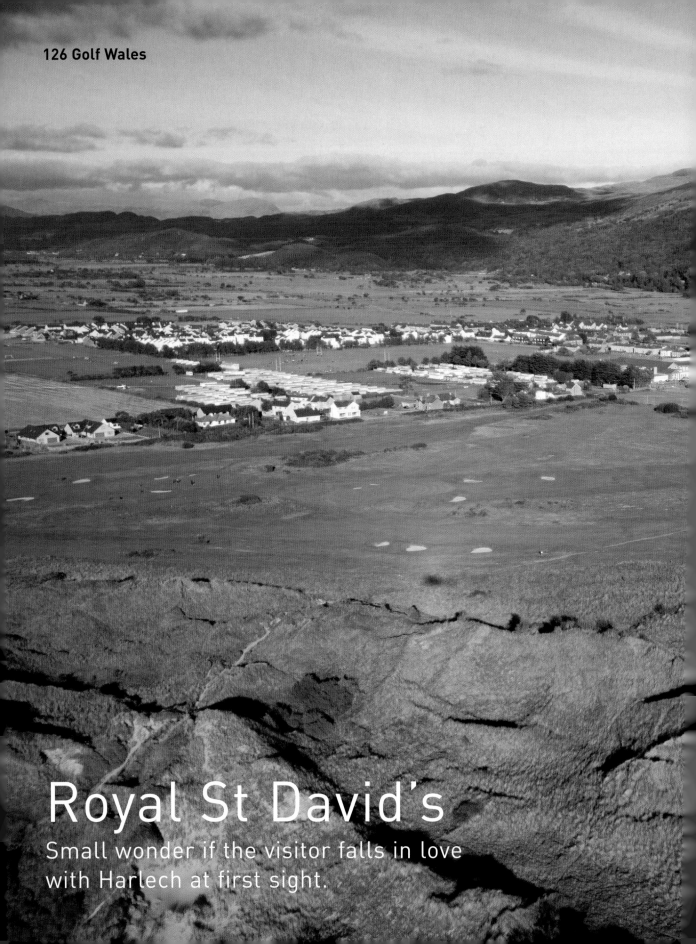

Royal St David's
Small wonder if the visitor falls in love
with Harlech at first sight.

Royal St David's Golf Club
18 hole, Par 69 (6,601 yds)
Links course.

While it would be over-egging the pudding to suggest that one royal club, Hoylake, would not be the club it is today had it not been for another, Harlech, it is not too far wide of the mark to observe that Royal St David's might not be the force it now is in golf without the support of members of Royal Liverpool. Harold Hilton and John Ball, the two amateurs who won the Open, were pillars of the club on the Wirral, and both travelled regularly to mid-Wales to play golf. Hilton's name appears as having won the Town Bowl in 1901 and 1902 and that of John Ball the Edward VII Bowl in 1920.

...the Harlech I played in the summer of 2006 was much the same as the Harlech I had played in the Welsh Boys' Championship in 1961 (I lost in the quarter-finals but thank you for asking).

It may be hard to imagine now but Harlech was quite a resort in Edwardian Britain. In his book *Every Day Was Summer*, the writer Oliver Wynne Hughes paints an evocative picture of a thriving resort which, because it was only 100 or so miles and a couple of hours by train from Liverpool and Manchester and 150 from Birmingham, seemed as glamorous then as many a continental resort.

The modern-day visitor will probably drive to Harlech but it is possible to get there by train as well. One alights at the station, walks a short distance, crosses the railway line and enters the Royal St David's golf club. "Small wonder if the visitor falls in love with Harlech at first sight, for no golf course in the world has a more splendid background than the old castle, which stands at

the top of a sheer precipice of rock looking down over the links," wrote Bernard Darwin in *Golf Courses of the British Isles*.

The club's reach throughout the game is considerable, and you get a sense that it is no ordinary club the moment you open its Strokesaver guide and see the advertisement on the inside facing page: it's for Bollinger champagne. Page 7 of the same guide contains an advertisement for the Raffles Resort on Canouan Island in The Grenadines. A handwritten letter on the clubhouse noticeboard is from Michael Lunt thanking the club for its congratulations extended to him when he became captain of the R & A in 2006.

So little has changed at Harlech. Other clubs buy more land, move tees, build new bunkers, alter the shape of holes, extend the clubhouse, lengthen the course but the Harlech I played in the summer of 2006 was much the same as the Harlech I had played in the Welsh Boys' Championship in 1961 (I lost in the quarter-finals but thank you for asking). >

Above: Harlech Castle dominates the golf course.

Its length from the men members' tees is a shade less than 6,500 yards and as a result you could be forgiven for thinking it a short course. Noting the five par 3s, including, unusually, the 18th, you might think it an insubstantial test. Look more closely however and you notice there are only two par 5s, which come one after the other, that one of the par 4s (the 3rd) is 463 yards and that on the homeward nine there are five par 4s of more than 425 yards. One last thing: the short holes play to the points of the compass so if, for example, the 11th is playing downwind, the 18th will be into the wind, if the 4th and the 9th are into the wind, there will be a slight respite on the 14th.

Should it be windy then gird yourself and be prepared for one of the hardest par 69s you will ever play.

Links courses cannot defend themselves solely with narrow fairways and enormous length and undulating greens because if the wind blows then such courses could be unplayable. So say a thank you should you catch Harlech, with its large and relatively

flat greens, on a benign day. Should it be windy then gird yourself
and be prepared for one of the hardest par 69s you will ever play.

It is an oddity for a seaside course that it is not until the
16th tee that the sea is sighted.

It is unoriginal to describe Royal St David's as a wolf in sheep's
clothing but that is precisely what it is. It is an oddity for a
seaside course that it is not until the 16th tee that the sea is
sighted. You can hear it rumbling and sighing just over the
sandhills but it only comes into view once - and then only for the
drive.

Forty years ago I felt that after the opening holes the course
softened slightly both in appearance and test as it meandered
away from the links-like soil of the first few holes towards the
turn where you could easily imagine yourself to be at Formby with
its stands of fir and pine trees. And my feelings remained the
same when I revisited the course recently. I felt that the first >

Above: The rugged beauty
and narrow fairways are well
demonstrated on the 15th.

four holes were demanding and appropriate to the terrain, that the next four were marginally less heroic and that from the 9th onwards you had better be paying attention otherwise a scorecard could be wrecked.

There is allure but no mystery as to the founding of Royal St David's on the flat acres that make up most of the land once covered by the sea beneath Edward I's imposing castle and between the railway line and Cardigan Bay. The allure is provided by the name of the man considered to be the club's founder: Harold Finch-Hatton, a younger brother of Dennis, who later featured in the film "Out of Africa".

W.H. Moore, the crown agent for Merionethshire, was walking on the Morfa one morning in the early 1890s when he saw Finch-Hatton throwing a boomerang, a skill he had acquired in Australia. Moore was intrigued and even more so when the next day he saw Finch-Hatton practising his golf on the Morfa. Moore did not know what golf was but it did not take long for him to realise its appeal. A telegram was sent to Finch-Hatton who replied, memorably, "Hold hard, coming tomorrow, have plan of course." The rest is history.

"We're a little local golf club with an international membership," David Morkill, the club secretary, remarked one stifling hot summer's day in 2006.

"One of our problems is getting local members because after people have grown up they tend to leave the area. If you looked through the early records of the club you would have seen that many of the members had addresses in London. But we started

international membership five years ago and we're thriving as never before. Three of our members have a plus handicap. We are the second club for Tim Dykes, the Wales international. As a matter of fact he won the club championship here yesterday with rounds of 68 and 71."

A telegram was sent to Finch-Hatton who replied, memorably, "Hold hard, coming tomorrow, have plan of course." The rest is history.

It is a matter of opinion whether Royal Porthcawl is a better test than Royal St David's. A rivalry has always existed between Wales's two clubs with the royal assent but it does not diminish from the charms, the tests and the characters of either of them. Wales is lucky to have them.

Above: Playing from the 8th fairway with Moelwyn Mawr behind.

At Harlech, you are never far
from Snowdonia's mountains.

Southerndown

...200 feet above sea level, has some rocky
outcrops among its downland soil and is near
the Merthyr Mawr sand dunes.

Southerndown Golf Club
18 hole, Par 70 (6,449 yds)
Downland/Links course.

A handful of golf clubs in Wales are inseparable in the way that their history is as famous and far-reaching as their course is distinguished. Their footprints in golf are large and powerful. Royal St David's and Royal Porthcawl will fight to be pre-eminent in such a list but also included in this group are Aberdovey, Southerndown and Ashburnham.

Any essay about Southerndown must detail the influence and involvement with the club of one of Wales's greatest golfing families, if not *the* greatest. Without the Duncans there might have been a Southerndown, though that is debatable, but without them it would not have achieved its current prominence. Without the Duncans there certainly would not have been a Duncan Putter.

The Duncans were an extraordinary family. Four of them won a total of 14 national championships in Wales – Colonel Tony Duncan, the men's four times, Blanche, his aunt, the women's five times, John, his father, the men's twice, and Margery, Tony's mother, the women's three times. John Duncan, a founding member of Southerndown, was the managing director of the family firm that published the South Wales News, a morning paper, and the South Wales Echo, an evening paper.

When Tony was 15, in 1929, the family left Cardiff to move to Southerndown. Later the family moved again, this time to St Nicholas, halfway between Southerndown and Cardiff. Regular visitors to the family home included Raymond Oppenheimer and Gerald Micklem, two massive figures in the game. Also Bernard Darwin came to stay at the time of the Wales v New Zealand rugby international in 1936. "It was the rubber match because Wales had won in 1905 and New Zealand in 1924," Tony Duncan recalled. "Bernardo got terribly excited and when Wales won he

took off the hat of the man sitting in front, who was a total stranger, and threw it in the air."

"The Duncan Putter gets its name from the putter that my father used for many years," Duncan told me one day when I was researching the history of the Welsh Golfing Union (which appeared on 11 January 1995 to mark the founding of the Union one hundred years to the day earlier). "It has a hickory shaft, is very upright and has two special marks on it, six inches apart. That was because in the old days when the stymie was in play you were allowed to lift if the balls were within six inches of one another. The scorecards were six inches wide but my father didn't trust them to be accurate so he had these marks made on his putter."

For a while the Duncan Putter was the first event on the amateur circuit each year and its list of winners bears out what an important event it was: Gordon Huddy (1959, 1961), Warren Humphreys (1971), Peter McEvoy (1978, 1980 and 1985), Stephen Dodd (1988), Stuart Manley (2002, 2003) and Nigel Edwards >

Above: "Here is the place for the purist who likes his golf strong and neat but doesn't mind a splash of hidden hazard."

• • • • • • • • • • • • • • • • •

(2004), all of whom played in the Walker Cup, and Peter Townsend (1965) and Phillip Price (1984) who played in the Ryder Cup. It remains a fixture on the calendar with, if anything, stronger fields now even if there are fewer star names.

These days Southerndown's distinctive feature is the sound of bleating sheep, a reminder that farmland adjoins the course, which is laid out on common land.

Southerndown, like Royal Porthcawl and Pyle and Kenfig, is laid out on land that is geologically unusual. Porthcawl, about as close to the sea as it is possible to get, has both sand-based, classic links land but also some moorland holes and Pyle and Kenfig is similar. Southerndown, on the other hand, is 200 feet above sea level, has some rocky outcrops among its downland soil and is near the Merthyr Mawr sand dunes. It is different in that a windblown acidic layer on top of a limestone base has given rise to an unusual limestone heath. "In one way the course is rather singular," Darwin wrote of Southerndown in his *Golf Courses of the British Isles*. "Being high in the air and not down on the level of the shore, it has many of the characteristics of the typical downland courses. It has their big rolling slopes and deep gullies but it has not, curiously to relate, the typical down turf."

The distinctive feature of Southerndown was once its astonishing length. In 1905, Willie Fernie, a lesser cousin of his more famous namesake, the 1883 Open champion, unveiled plans for a 7,170-yard course on Ogmore Downs, the longest in the United Kingdom at a time when the Old Course at St Andrews measured 6,323

yards, Muirfield 5,829 and Prestwick 5,732 yards. A correspondent in the *Daily Chronicle* suggested "there was not very much to be proud of in the matter....Of the new course there are seven holes of 500 yards or over....What a place for the player who is a little off with his wooden clubs!"

it's a golfers' golf course, hard work, hard walking and thoroughly rewarding for all that...

These days Southerndown's distinctive feature is the sound of bleating sheep, a reminder that farmland adjoins the course, which is laid out on common land. Sheep seem to be nibbling at the fringes of so many of its greens. It's an up hill, down dale sort of course, with more ferns than necessary and remarkable views from most holes. It's a golfer's golf course: hard work, hard walking and thoroughly rewarding for all that; the sort of course that makes you think to yourself at times "is there much more of this" but which you are pleased to have finished. It leaves you with a feeling of physical well-being and triumph. >

Above: Southerdown's greens are well defended by bunkers as demonstrated here on the 2nd.

● ● ● ● ● ● ● ● ● ● ● ● ● ● ● ●

If Southerndown were a man, it would be large and craggy-faced, all knees and elbows. When the wind blows (and up there, when does it not?) it is a tartar of a course. "Here is the place for the purist who likes his golf strong and neat but doesn't mind a splash of hidden hazard," George Houghton wrote in *Golf Addict invades Wales* and though some features of the course now look a touch dated, it remains a severe test at a shade under 6,500 yards from the back tees.

It is just the sort of windy and demanding course that breeds champions and it might have entitled its club history *Mighty Winds...Mighty Champions* as Royal Liverpool did. As well as producing nearly 25 men internationals for Wales, some of whom also played for Great Britain and Ireland, Southerndown has developed more than its share of women golfers. Its latest stars are Anna Highgate, a Curtis Cup player in 2004 and Amy Rees. Nor should we forget Llewellyn Matthews, the 2006 Welsh Amateur champion.

Above: Henry Cotton described the 1st as "One of the most difficult opening holes in golf!"

 ...a drive on the 17th by Peter Croke, a club member, hit a sheep and implanted itself in the animal's bottom. Startled (and can one wonder?) the sheep ran up the fairway and deposited the ball 30 yards nearer the hole from where Croke got down in 5 and won the hole.

In 1995 the club found itself in the news for none of the aforementioned reasons but instead for the fact that a drive on the 17th by Peter Croke, a club member, hit a sheep and implanted itself in the animal's bottom. Startled (and can one wonder?) the sheep ran up the fairway and deposited the ball 30 yards nearer the hole from where Croke got down in 5 and won the hole. >

● ● ● ● ● ● ● ● ● ● ● ● ● ● ● ●

Croke, however, was reprimanded by the late John Glover, then a rules expert at the Royal and Ancient Golf Club of St Andrews. "Under rule 19-1A, if a ball in motion after a stroke comes to rest in an inanimate outside agency (the sheep) the player shall drop the ball as near as possible to the spot where the sheep was when the ball came to rest in it," Glover wrote. "The ball may be cleaned. Contrary to the report, the player did not proceed properly and his opponent could have claimed the hole. I feel a little sheepish about bringing this to your attention but felt that matters should be put right."

What can you learn about a club from its clubhouse? I submit that the architecture and ambience of a clubhouse are a part of its DNA and nearly as revealing. The one at Southerndown is homely, warm and distinctive, a bit like the one at Ashburnham, another of the aristocracy among Wales's golf clubs. As you glimpse the Southerndown clubhouse in the distance from one of the closing holes, it looks squat and sturdy, indestructible even, completely at one with its surroundings. On wet and windy days, it is a welcoming sight indeed. ●

Above: The Ogmore river valley adds to the distractions on the 1st tee.

Right: The squat and sturdy clubhouse.. a welcoming sight indeed.

As you glimpse the Southerndown clubhouse in the distance from one of the closing holes, it looks squat and sturdy, indestructible even, completely at one with its surroundings. On wet and windy days, it is a welcoming sight, indeed.

The 5th hole is known as
'Carter's folly' after
Brigadier General Carter
who had a hand in its design.

Tenby

There are longer courses that are less challenging and shorter courses that are more difficult but Tenby is both fun and difficult.

Tenby Golf Club
18 hole, Par 68 (6,026 yds)
Links course.

When you are in your car and moving slowly down Weston Street or Warren Street in Tenby you can have no idea there is a golf course anywhere near you. Driving towards the railway station you have things on your mind other than that within a few hundred yards you can be on the 1st tee of the oldest, most sporty course in Wales. All around you are shops, houses, cars, lorries and bustling people. How can there possibly be a golf course nearby?

I find it refreshing to think that you can leave a town centre hotel with your clubs over your back and walk to a golf club.

But just as I like my rugby grounds to be within walking distance of a city centre, which makes the Millennium Stadium in Cardiff one of my favourites and Lansdowne Road in Dublin another, so I find it refreshing to think that you can leave a town centre hotel with your clubs over your back and walk to a golf club. St Andrews is the best example of this but Tenby comes close. Turn right out of the Imperial Hotel, walk for five minutes and you are there. The Burrows was not designed with golf in mind but it might have been. It has springy turf, soft underfoot, as well as high sand dunes and wonderful views across Carmarthen Bay.

These are things I like about Tenby:

– that it is accepted as being Wales's oldest course, being one of the clubs invited to attend a meeting on 11 January 1895 at the Raven Hotel in Shrewsbury at which it was proposed and seconded that "A Welsh Golfing Union be now formed." Tenby scorecards bear the legend "The Oldest Affiliated Golf Club in Wales". I also like the story that in 1875 the Mayor of Tenby chose to abandon a case in court because he wanted to play golf.

- that its holes are named after a person or an object or a piece of history. Thus Dai Rees is the name of the 3rd because the great Welsh golfer took a particular fancy to this hole. One day I watched a man aim a putt towards St Catherine Island in the Bay to allow for the contours of the green; it was like watching a golfer putt towards 1 o'clock when his target was 5 o'clock. Penally Butts is now the name of the 8th because the rifle range is to the right of this hole. Monk's Way refers to the path the monks took across what is now the golf course, on their way to Caldey Island. The 18th is named after Dr Charles Mathias, a bigwig at the club between the wars who designed the humps to the right of the 18th green. The humps became known as Charlie's Whiskers.

- that there are so few bunkers, a reminder that this course was laid out in the days when horses, pulling earth-moving equipment, were the conventional means of scraping out a bunker. More than a century ago excavating a bunker was hard work and clubs kept this sort of work to a minimum. At Royal Ashdown Forest in Sussex for example, laid out only a few >

Above: At night Tenby Harbour could easily be mistaken for a port on the Continent.

● ● ● ● ● ● ● ● ● ● ● ● ● ● ● ● ●

years after Tenby, there is not a single bunker on the course.

- that its greens are very close to its tees, another sign that it was built a long time ago. As is the rusty bell between the 4th green and the 5th tee (which gives the 4th its name), as are the old-fashioned boxes on each tee containing divot mix, the wooden bench at the back of the 12th tee and finally, the way that from the 7th tee you could probably lean over and hand a cup of tea to a passing train driver. Oh yes, and that the 6th is known as Lifter's Cottage because it was the home of the people who operated the railway crossing gates.

- that its sportiness presents a challenge. There are longer courses that are less challenging and shorter courses that are more difficult but Tenby is fun and difficult. Try playing the 12th in an on-shore wind. Imagine yourself to be two or three strokes within your handicap when you are playing the 18th. Feel any pressure not to hook the ball with the fence and the railway line down the left? Bet you do.

Above: Players ring a bell upon leaving the 4th green, set down in a dell. Hence the hole's nickname – "The Bell".

- that while you have a hint of the sea at the start of your round, it only becomes noticeable if you climb the dunes to the left of the 4th. There in the distance is Caldey Island and the Monastery.

Imagine yourself to be two or three strokes within your handicap when you are playing the 18th. Feel any pressure not to hook the ball with the fence and the railway line down the left? Bet you do."

As soon as you turn into Station Road you see the railway line and suddenly memories of Aberdovey and Harlech in Wales, Turnberry and Troon in Scotland, of Royal Lytham & St Annes and Formby in England come to mind. Would golf on these courses have grown the way it has if golfers had not been delivered by trains practically to the 1st tee? Lytham made its name because the industrial barons of Manchester wanted somewhere to go for weekends – and something to do when they got there. Turnberry used to receive trains full of revellers up from London on a >

● ● ● ● ● ● ● ● ● ● ● ● ● ● ●

Friday night. The trains would turn around on the turntable outside the foyer of the hotel (the shape of which is still visible) and transport the revellers back to London on Sunday evening.

The 1st at Tenby goes away from the clubhouse down an isthmus of land bounded by the railway on one side and scrub on the other. From this, the first-time visitor is entitled to expect the course to be compact. But then you cross the path behind the 1st green, walk a few steps to the 2nd tee and suddenly some of Tenby's scale is there before you.

The 2nd and 3rd holes take you out towards the end of the course and bring you back almost to where you were a moment ago. Then you head out once more and so you make your way zig-zagging across the land. The only slight disappointment are the 15th, 16th and 17th holes over the railway line, though plans are afoot to redesign the course to have every hole on the seaward side of the railway line. Rather like the last three holes at Conwy, the current 15th, 16th and 17th are not of a piece with the rest of the course and it is a relief to cross the railway line again and reach the 18th tee near where the old clubhouse used to be. From there you can look at the new clubhouse in the distance and know that your round is nearly over and well played or badly played, you will soon be home. ●

Opposite: The sweep of the bay, a sandy beach, a lonely golfer beneath a clear sky – the delights of golf at Tenby.

The 5th is named 'Swn y Môr' (sound of the sea) due to its proximity to the beach.

Where to eat and stay

Good quality food and accommodation is pretty important after a gruelling 18 holes so the the following few pages provide a guide to some of the best places to stay and eat in close proximity to our featured courses. Colin Pressdee provides a synopsis of his first hand experiences in some of his preferred places and invites us to share some of his favourite foods.

Colin Pressdee

Colin Pressdee is a food writer, broadcaster and consultant. His most recent book Food Wales, published in 2005 has gained high acclaim as a comprehensive guide of where to find, taste and buy Welsh food. He wrote the first Dining Out in Wales Guide in 2004 featuring the top 150 restaurants in Wales.

He wrote the food, wine and restaurant pages for the Western Mail Magazine and Wales on Sunday for over a decade, winning a Glenfiddich Award as Regional Writer of the Year in 1990. Currently he writes the wine column for the Daily Post and contributes food and travel articles to various newspapers and magazines.

He presented Hedgerow Harvest on UKTV Great Food Live in 2005; the food on BBC Wales See You Sunday 1990-93; similarly for BBC 2 Summer Scene broadcast from the Garden Festival at Ebbw vale in 1992; and Night Bites for ITV during 1995-6. He has written two recipe books to complement series on BBC Radio Wales: Streetwise Cookery in 1992 and Welsh Coastal Cookery in 1995.

Born in Mumbles and brought up on the Gower Peninsula he is a keen bass, crab and lobster fisher. He enjoys country pursuits, particularly salmon, sewin and trout angling. He is passionate about conservation and the environment. He is interested in the provenance of organic and natural food from land and sea, particularly shellfish, game and artisan cheeses. He undertook a project for the sustainable use of natural foods from woodlands and hedgerows in 2006 for Northern Marches Cymru.

Colin now lives in London but maintains close ties with Wales. He works with hotels and organic food companies, helping to publicise fine Welsh organic produce to wholesalers, retailers and restaurateurs in London.

Contents

Aberdovey

1. Bistro on the Square
1 Chapel Square, Aberdovey,
Gwynedd LL35 0SB
Tel: 01654 767448

Literally on the square in the town centre this comfortable bistro offers honest food and honest prices. There is an impressive choice of vegetarian dishes such as baked red onion and aubergine tart, and butternut squash filled with fried vegetables, couscous and cheese. The catch of the day is listed on a chalkboard and might be mackerel, bass, plaice or mullet. Similarly meat lovers can select various steaks, or try tenderloin of pork, rack of lamb, Gressingham duck or guinea fowl. Prices are most reasonable throughout.

Personal favourite
• Smoked haddock dauphinoise
• Mrs Pharoah's (snr) chicken pie

2. Wynnstay
Maengwyn Street,
Machynlleth,
Powys SY20 8AE
Tel: 01654 702941
Fax: 01654 703884
E: info@wynnstay-hotel.com
www.wynnstay-hotel.com

From Aberdovey: 10.5 miles

This large coaching inn is in the centre of the ancient capital of Wales. The bar is set for informal food by a roaring fire with several separate dining rooms and lounges with a variety of menus. A pizzeria across the courtyard has been judged the best in Britain showing the Celtic-Italian influence that carries through all the cuisine. Prime Welsh ingredients have a local or Italian treatment, with cockles and laverbread alongside tagliata and pestun, both Ligurian specialities. Regional Italian wines shine.

Personal favourite
• Linguini with cockles
• Middle White pork with spiced apples and black pudding

3. Ynyshir Hall
Eglwysfach, Nr Machynlleth,
Powys SY20 8TA
Tel: 01654 781209
Fax: 01654 781366
E: info@ynyshirhall.co.uk
www.ynyshir-hall.co.uk

From Aberdovey: 16.5 miles

A beautiful Georgian country house in acres of rolling parkland is the setting for grand cuisine. The colourful paintings of local scenes are matched by the flamboyance of the food and ambience. The food aims to be at the heart of modern gastronomy and dedication to detail is impeccable. Cardigan Bay seafood and Welsh mountain lamb are treated with equal respect and flavours come through as positively as the colours in the artist's work. A comprehensive wine list backs up the grand style.

Personal favourite
• Veal sweetbreads with cinnamon apple puree
• Crisp skinned bass with scallop stuffed courgette flower,
  fennel puree

Penmaenuchaf Hall | Mackerel | Penhelig Arms

4. Penmaenuchaf Hall

Penmaenpool, Dolgellau,
Gwynedd LL40 1YB
Tel: 01341 422129
Fax: 01341 422787
www.penhall.co.uk
E:relay@penhall.co.uk

From Aberdovey: 27 miles

This Victorian mansion overlooking the Mawddach Estuary has a warm welcoming ambience. The comfortable panelled dining room is pristine and elegant. The food is carefully sourced from local suppliers, so expect fresh plaice, salmon and sewin, plus fine lamb and beef from the renowned butcher in Bala, and local game in season. Cooking is highly competent without being over fussy matching flavours and cooking techniques with skill. Their wine club ensures that the selection is comprehensive at very fair prices.

Personal favourite
• Braised monkfish with asparagus, lemon and dill dressing
• Best end of welsh lamb with swede confit, lentils and rosemary

5. Penhelig Arms Hotel and Restaurant

Terrace Road, Aberdovey,
Gwynedd LL35 0LT
Tel: 01654 767215
Fax: 01654 767690
E:info@penheligarms.com
www.penheligarms.com

This pristine inn on the sea front has enchanting views over the estuary and salt marshes. The public bar is the hub of the area with great atmosphere and truly tasty food, taking in a wide range of familiar ingredients. The restaurant has the style of a bistro de luxe. There's local crab and lobster in season, plus a wide range of fish, together with a comprehensive meat offering. The wine list is amazing running to hundreds of bins and at bargain prices.

Personal favourite
• Fillet of mackerel with chilli, ginger and garlic
• Braised lamb shank in red wine and winter vegetables

Ashburnham

Parc Howard Museum and Art Gallery, Llanelli

Nantgaredig **2**

4 Llansteffan

Ashburnham

Loughor **6**

1 **3** **5**

Llanrhidian Swansea

1. The Welcome to Town

Llanrhidian, Gower SA3 1EH
Tel: 01792 390015
www.thewelcometotown.co.uk

From Ashburnham: 19 miles

This former local pub is now a restaurant specialising in food from Gower. The cooking is highly competent in the treatment of both meat and seafood. The menu features salt marsh lamb from the Bury Estuary a few hundred yards away, plus cockles and laverbread from the sea beyond. Gower lobster excels grilled with beurre blanc sauce, and equally fresh are other fish such as sewin and bass. It's very good value, this extending across the concise wine list.

Personal favourite
- Laverbread in an overcoat of scrambled eggs
- Pannacotta with rhubarb compote and biscotti

2. Y Polyn

Nantgaredig,
Carmarthenshire
SA32 7LH
Tel: 01267 290000
www.ypolyn.com

From Ashburnham: 20.7 miles

This black and white former local pub is built over a stream. The bar and restaurant has simple décor with local Artist's paintings, pine furniture and is the setting for some very accomplished cooking. Welsh produce features highly on the menu, much of it sourced from Carmarthenshire or Pembrokeshire. Some dishes are traditional such as potted shrimps and fish pie, while others push the boundaries, drawing on traditional French styles. Welsh farmhouse cheeses feature alongside home made desserts.

Personal favourite
- Rilettes of organic Carmarthenshire pork with peach chutney
- Walnut crusted goats' cheese with beetroot salad

3. Hurrens

Hurrens Inn on the Estuary
13 Station Road, Loughor,
Swansea SA4 6TR
Tel: 01792 899092

From Ashburnham: 9.5 miles

The inn on the estuary overlooks the Loughor River and west to the vast Bury inlet. Its slogan of simply great food, wine and real ales makes it highly popular with locals. The menu takes in a wide range of styles with a touch of Italian, French, Cajun and Eastern applied to items such as wild boar, duck breast, Welsh steaks, pork, bream, mullet and halibut. Portions are generous and come with vegetables and potatoes. Home made desserts and Welsh cheeses complete the bountiful menu.

Personal favourite
- Pan fried calf's liver with red onion marmalade
- Pork saltimbocca with rocket salad

Pheasant · Welcome to Town Inn · Lavabread

4. Yr Hen Dafarn, Ferryside

Llansteffan,
Carmarthenshire,
SA33 5JY
Tel: 01267 241656

From Ashburnham: 21.7 miles

The black and white former pub will open for bookings and is well worthy of the drive to the other side of the estuary. The décor is basic, the service and cooking by the proprietors, and the fare can be memorable. In the summer there will be loads of fresh seafoods, much caught by owner Bill himself. In the winter he shoots and brings in anything from venison to mallard and woodcock. Vegetables are from the garden, wines are very inexpensive and a jolly evening is certain.

Personal favourite
• Pheasant casserole
• Grilled Pembroke crawfish or lobster

5. The Restaurant @ Pilot House Wharf

Pilot House Wharf, Trawler Road,
Swansea SA1 1UN
Tel: 01792 466200

From Ashburnham: 18.5 miles

Fishing gear and old prints of Swansea ships greet you on the staircase to this restaurant overlooking the River Tawe barrage and the quay where trawlers berth. Neat with pine furniture the food takes advantage of local landings, and the abundance of produce in Swansea market. The menu includes several meat dishes, particularly Welsh lamb. Cooking is straightforward and accurate with well made sauces such as hollandaise, beurre blanc or chilli jam. There are delicious desserts and reasonable wine.

Personal favourite
• Deep fried squid with chilli jam
• Roasted hake with asparagus and hollandaise

6. Morgans

Somerset Place, Swansea SA1 1RR
Tel: 01792 484848 Fax: 01792 484849
E: reception@morganshotel.co.uk
www.morganshotel.co.uk

From Ashburnham: 17.3 miles

This hotel is in the tastefully converted former Swansea Docks Board offices. The majestic building has grand proportions and is the first in-city boutique hotel, complete with luxurious furnishings and up to date technology. Dine in this elegance on local fare sourced from Swansea Market and the area. Specialities include locally landed fish, such as Gower bass and Towy sewin, salt marsh lamb from the Bury Estuary, and true Welsh specialities of Penclawdd cockles and laverbread. Enjoy the Champagne Bar for pre and post meal drinks.

Celtic Manor

1. Owens

Celtic Manor Resort,
Coldra Woods, Newport,
Gwent NP18 1HQ
Tel: 01633 413000
Fax: 01633 412910
E: bookings@celtic-manor.com
E: postbox@celtic-manor.com
www.Celtic-manor.com

The magnificent Celtic Manor has several restaurants including the informal Olive Tree Restaurant and the sophisticated Owen's Fine Dining restaurant. The latter is for seriously good food in elegant modern surroundings. The menu certainly focuses on prime Welsh ingredients such as Pembroke crab, Carmarthen ham, Welsh Black beef, salt marsh lamb, Welsh cheeses. These are presented in complex dishes with many layers of flavours and ingredients. Desserts too have many different treatments to complete the gastronomic blow out.

Personal favourite
- Welsh salt marsh lamb with lemongrass risotto
- The Collection of miniature desserts

2. The Foxhunter

Nant-y-Derry, Abergavenny,
Monmouthshire NP7 9DN
Tel: 01873 881101
Fax: 01873 881377
E: info@thefoxhunter.com
www.thefoxhunter.com

From Celtic Manor: 17.8 miles

This former Victorian station pub now has sophisticated contemporary décor blended with original features. Solid beech furniture sits on a Welsh flagstone floor. It's the setting for highly competent cuisine that's earned many accolades. Menus and dishes are concise, confident and combine pristine ingredients. Expect wild bass, Brecon venison, Longhorn beef, perhaps home picked mushrooms, country style terrine, hot damsons on toast and fine British and French cheeses. Well selected wines complement the food style, making the entire experience a joy.

Personal favourite
- Tagliatelle of braised rabbit and parmesan
- Scottish sea trout, sweet and sour tomato dressing and sea spinach

3. The Hardwick

Old Raglan Road, Abergavenny,
Monmouthshire NP7 9AA
Tel: 01873 854220

From Celtic Manor: 24.5 miles

It's a quick drive to the outskirts of Abergavenny to the Hardwick, a restaurant in a former pub. The extensive menu is executed with skill from a very competent kitchen. Lunch offers a selection of gourmet sandwiches with triple cooked chips, as an alternative to the main menu. Innovative use of prime ingredients such as Gloucester Old Spot pork, Brixham crab and Hereford beef, with garnishes such as Amalfi lemons, cavolo nero cabbage, polenta and lentils gives a sophisticated continental style to skilfully presented dishes.

Personal favourite
- Ironbark pumpkin, Jerusalem artichoke, red onion and goats' cheese rotolo with an Italian spinach, trevise lettuce toasted pumpkin seed and pine nut salad

Pork selection at Owens

Owens Restaurant

4. The Newbridge
Tredunnock, Nr Usk,
Monmouthshire NP15 1LY
Tel: 01633 451000
Fax: 01633 451001
www.thenewbridge.co.uk

From Celtic Manor: 4.7 miles

This spacious, beautifully appointed restaurant has comfortable bars in several areas with an open gallery on the first floor linking an overall ambience. The terrace and garden menu offers inexpensive bistro style dishes such as beer battered fish and chips, salads, pasta and grills. The main menu has Tidenham Chase chicken and duck, Bwlch venison, Monmouthshire lamb and fish chalked daily on a board as delivered from Cornwall. Cooking is competent, presentations delightful, and wines fairly priced.

Personal favourite
- Cornish lobster on mango salad with citrus dressing
- Saddle of Bwlch venison with dauphinoise potatoes and Savoy cabbage

5. Chandlery Restaurant
77–78 Lower Dock Street,
Newport, Gwent NP20 1EH
Tel: 01633 256622
Fax: 01633 256633
www.chandleryrestaurant.co.uk

From Celtic Manor: 4 miles

This smart Georgian town building has clean contemporary décor and a youthful team running a very sophisticated kitchen. A bargain lunch menu has mouth watering dishes such as crab and fennel linguini, braised shoulder of lamb with polenta and aubergine, and 'free range' faggots and pork sausages. Evenings enjoy saffron risotto and fried monkfish, duck and apple terrine, Welsh mountain lamb, pheasant, calves liver, yellow fin tuna on a sensible concise menu with delicious flavour combinations. Wines are good value.

Personal favourite
- Cornish bass, crab mash, shellfish and sweet corn chowder
- Mature Welsh Black sirloin, beef ragout, celeriac mash, herb crust

6. The Angel Hotel
15 Cross Street,
Abergavenny NP7 5EN
T: 01873 857121
F: 01873 858059
E:reservation@angelhotelabergavenny.com
www.angelhotelabergavenny.com

From Celtic Manor: 25.5 miles

This large town hotel has been beautifully refurbished with modern features mingling with traditional. Meals are served in the comfortable bar and the large dining room. Lunch includes a range of sandwiches. Organic vegetables are noted on the menu alongside Black Mountain smoked produce, Gloucester Old Spot pork, Welsh lamb, wild bass, organic salmon, scallops and mussels. Local beef comes as burger or 28day matured steak. Cooking is very competent and presented with style. The well referenced wine list is very fairly priced.

Personal favourite
- Free range chicken with wild mushroom stuffing
- New England pumpkin cake, caramel sauce, chocolate parfait

Conwy

1. The Queen's Head & Storehouse Cottage

Glanwydden, Conwy LL31 9JP
Tel: 01492 546570
Fax: 01492 546487
E:enquiries@queensheadglanwydden.co.uk
www.queensheadglanwydden.co.uk

From Conwy: 4.9 miles

This smart white pub in the tiny village has been a food destination for many years. It is run very efficiently, the staff are very attentive and it is always very busy. Dining extends through several cosy rooms with warming fires in winter. The menu is packed with local produce and the style is developing all the time with dishes for hearty eaters, fish lovers, carnivores and vegetarians. Forty wines are sensibly priced and well described.

Personal favourite
• Roasted butternut squash and chestnut risotto
• Queen's Head smokie

2. Castle Hotel

High Street, Conwy LL32 8DB
Tel: 01492 582800
Fax: 01492 582300
E: mail@castlelwales.co.uk
www.castlewales.co.uk

From Conwy: 1.1 miles

This magnificent town hotel offers highly competent cuisine either in Shakespeare's restaurant or in the less formal atmosphere of Dawson's bar. There are many familiar modish dishes and ingredients and plenty from the locale including Conwy mussels and crab. The restaurant menu has many quite complicated dishes for serious diners, while the bar has concise simpler food. There are mouth watering nibbles, fish chowder, eclectic dishes, grills and sizzling platters. The home made puddings and Welsh farmhouse cheeses are tempting to the end.

Personal favourite
• Ham hock terrine wrapped in air dried ham
• Posh fish and chips – scallops, salmon, king prawn, monkfish

3. Quay Hotel, Deganwy, Vue Restaurant

Quay Hotel and Spa
Deganwy Quay, Deganwy,
Conwy LL31 9DJ
Tel: 01492 564100 Fax: 01492 564115
E: enquiries@quayhotel.com
www.quayhotel.com

From Conwy: 2.8 miles

This brand new spa hotel on the quay has fine views over Conwy Estuary to the Castle and Penmeanmawr Mountain. The elevated restaurant is modern minimalism with great style. Star food comes from a highly competent team. The skilful combinations of ingredients are presented in contemporary style. A variety of cooking techniques applied to ingredients such as Conwy mussels, scallops, crab, bass, lamb, pork and beef with some modish and eclectic touches delivers many interesting dishes that will delight.

Personal favourite
• Scallop boudin, local mussels, basil bouillon
• Seared bass, tomato fondue, fennel crisps, vanilla mash

Tan Y Foel Welsh seafood Castle Hotel

4. Tan Y Foel

Capel Garmon, Nr Betws-y-Coed,
Conwy LL26 0RE
Tel: 01690 710507
Fax: 01690 710681
E:enquiries@tyfhotel.co.uk
www.tyfhotel.co.uk

Closed: Dec – Jan
From Conwy: 18.2 miles

If looking for a small dinner party for four, this little boutique hotel on the hills above the Conwy Valley offers something really special. The small daily changing menu has a choice of two per course. Each dish is carefully crafted using classic cooking techniques with intelligent combinations of ingredients to bring harmony to each dish. Fish might be turbot, bass, grey mullet or salmon, while meaty dishes include rabbit, duck, lamb, pork or veal. Desserts are equally impressive. A wine is confidently recommended with each course.

Personal favourite
• Seared fillet of smoked salmon, celeriac remoulade, salsa Verdi
• Turbot with mushroom herb crust, salmon tartare potato cake

5. Ty Gwyn Hotel

Betws-y-Coed, Conwy LL25 0SG
Tel: 01690 710383

From Conwy: 21 miles

Adjacent to the famous Waterloo Bridge over the River Conwy this black and white cottage hotel has warm fabrics, homely comfortable chairs, oak beams, brasses and copper bric a brac and warm fires. Dining extends from the bar to several interconnecting rooms. A lengthy blackboard menu includes lots of seafood including Conwy mussels, crab and bass, plus meaty offerings including bison steak and game. It changes with seasons and cooking is competent with hearty portions with real ales and inexpensive wines.

Personal favourite
• Local ceps with shallots, tumeric and cream
• Pheasant casserole

6. St Tudno

Promenade, Llandudno,
Conwy LL30 2LP
Tel: 01492 874411
F: 01492 860407
E:sttudno@btinterent.com
www.st-tudno.co.uk

From Conwy: 5.5 miles

This is the gem among all the hotels on the Victorian seafront. Lounges have views over the bay and the Terrace Restaurant is discreet and hidden with relaxing country décor of a Victorian garden. The concise menu has intelligently composed dishes from prime ingredients. Items vary daily and change seasonally. Local bass, turbot, crab, venison, Welsh Black beef and lamb and a vegetarian choice present a good balance. Home made desserts excel and Welsh cheeses and Welsh rarebit round the meal in style.

Personal favourite
• Rare tuna with Nicoise salad, lemon confit and mustard cream
• White chocolate tulip with candied pineapple and coconut ice

Cradoc

Llangorse Lake

1. Felinfach Griffin

Felinfach, Nr Brecon,
Powys LD3 0UB
Tel: 01874 620111
Fax: 01874 620120
E: enquiries@eatdrinksleep.ltd.uk
www.eatdrinksleep.ltd.uk

From Cradoc: 7.8 miles

This inn offers 'eat, drink, sleep' and provides these with style. Many creature comforts include fires, an Aga, deep sofas and a warm dining area. The garden is used in the summer. The menu is based on rural produce but presented as a city gastro pub. Cooking is assertive and accurate. Game, pigeon, rabbit come in season with seafood more prominent in summer. Welsh lamb and beef excel; steak, béarnaise and chips being exemplary. Terrific, well priced wines and real ales.

Personal favourite
• Venison, autumn fruits, dauphinois potatoes
• Quail, puy lentils cep cappuccino

2. Peterstone Court

Llanhamlach, Brecon, Powys LD3 7YB
Tel: 01874 665387 Fax: 01874 665376
E: info@peterstone-court.com
www.peterstone-court.com

Nantyffin Cider Mill

Brecon Road, Crickhowell, Powys
NP8 1SG Tel: 01873 810775
E: info@cidermill.co.uk
www.cidermill.co.uk

A nearby family farm provides for the menus at the hotel and the Cider Mill lower down the Usk Valley. The old world pub (Nantyffin) serves fresh fish daily featuring perhaps scallops, lemon sole, bass, red mullet and hake. Slow cooking techniques with skill presents dishes such as confit of lamb or duck, and steamed beef and vegetable pudding, all come in hearty portions. The hotel's menu used many of the prime cuts and provides a more formal venue. Both have wonderful wine lists.

Personal favourite
• Canon of Glaisfer lamb with aubergine caviar and asparagus
• Roast guinea fowl, fondant potatoes, cider sauce

3. White Swan

Llanfrynach, Brecon,
Powys LD3 7BZ
Tel: 01874 665276
Fax: 01874 665362
www.the-white-swan.com

From Cradoc: 6.5 miles
Accommodation 1 mile from restaurant

The façade of a white washed terrace row of cottages hides the labyrinths inside and the wisteria clad terrace behind. This local pub is welcoming with its rich wood and leather furnishings and friendly staff. Locally sourced produce such as local lamb and Bwlch venison show their affinity with the area, together with daily fish specials. Dishes might mix styles of cuisine with plenty of innovation and these are popular with regulars. Wines are good value for the international selection.

Personal favourite
• Home smoked duck breast with beetroot, mango and pickled walnuts
• Haunch of Bwlch venison with offal faggot and sage mash

Peterstone Court

Bear

4. Bear

High Street, Crickhowell,
Powys NP8 1BW
Tel: 01873 810408 Fax: 01873 811696
E: bearhotel@aol.com
www.bearhotel.co.uk

From Cradoc: 16.7 miles

This fifteenth century coaching inn is the social hub of the small market town. The bar extends over several rooms, all with a feel of the original inn. An extensive menu is full of local foods from salmon and sewin in season to winter steamed game pudding. The beamed and flagstone restaurant oozes atmosphere and serves sophisticated country cooking with some slow roast dishes, fresh lobster in summer and homely style puddings. A wide selection of wine by the glass and real ales keeps this veritable hostelry packed.

Personal favourite
- Tartlet of quail with caramelised onions and quail's eggs
- Tournedos of monkfish with five spices, ragout of butter beans sweet corn and smoked bacon

5. Lake

Lake Country House & Spa
Llangammarch Wells, Powys LD4 4BS
Tel: 01591 620202
Fax: 01591 620457
E: info@lakecountryhouse.co.uk
www.lakecountryhouse.co.uk

From Cradoc: 15.9 miles

This magnificent black and white country house hotel with the new superb spa is a place for relaxation and very sophisticated dining. The dinner menu takes in some very fine ingredients including oysters, scallops, crab, turbot, Welsh Black beef, mountain lamb, duck and a selection of game in season. Cooking is intricate and presented in highly colourful striking combinations with elements of dishes carefully mingled together on each successive course. The fine wine cellar and professional relaxing service are both impressive.

Personal favourite
- Scallops with caramelised belly pork, crab and cinnamon tuile
- Roast squab with roast fig sauce, ravioli of parsnips, truffle foam, cep oil

Holyhead

Amlwch

Church Bay
Holyhead
Red Wharf Bay
Treaddur Bay
Beaumaris

1. Ship Inn

Red Wharf Bay,
Anglesey LL75 8RJ
Tel: 01248 852568
Fax: 01248 851013
www.shipinnredwharfbay.co.uk

From Holyhead: 24.9 miles

This old inn is set in a row of fishermen's cottages just above the high water mark of the sheltered bay. Interconnecting rooms have nautical décor on original stone walls and roaring fires in the winter. Summertime al fresco dining extends along an outside terrace. The menu has plenty of local seafood and meat from Anglesey including Welsh Black beef. Portions are hearty and puddings particularly of note include crème brulee and summer pudding.

Personal favourite
- Dressed Anglesey crab salad
- Grilled sewin with beurre blanc

2. Lobster Pot, Church Bay

Church Bay Nr Holyhead,
Anglesey LL65 4EU
Tel: 01407 730241
www.thelobsterpot.info

Closed: Nov-Mar
From Holyhead: 9.9 miles
Holiday cottages available

This was originally a tea room in the 1950s specialising in lobster teas. Now dining is in several rooms and sun lounges, with a children's play room and a spacious garden. The décor has changed little, some rooms with fishing artefacts. There's a wide choice of fresh seafood at very good prices as much comes from the lobster ponds next door, with fresh fish collected directly from local boats. Anglesey lamb and beef completes the offer. The wine list has many bargains including Cloudy Bay.

Personal favourite
- Holyhead scallops wrapped in streaky bacon
- Grilled lobster with garlic and parsley butter

3. Ye Olde Bull's Head

Castle Street, Beaumaris,
Anglesey LL58 8AP
Tel: 01248 810329
Fax: 01248 811294
E: info@bullsheadinn.co.uk
www.bullsheadinn.co.uk

From Holyhead: 23.6 miles

This fine old coaching inn has been discreetly modernised without losing any of its character. Serious evening dining is in the beamed restaurant where grand cuisine is based on locally sourced meat, fish and vegetables cooked with great skill. A modern brasserie extension on the ground floor serves an extensive menu from baguettes and salads to simply grilled fish and steaks, but all to a high standard. Both have interesting wines at fair prices including some from Henschke.

Personal favourite
- Terrine of skate with capers and gherkins
- Menai bass, salsify, ceps and beurre blanc

Crab

Ye Olde Bull's Head

4. Waterfront

Lon Isallt, Trearddur Bay,
Anglesey LL65 2UW
Tel: 01407 860006

From Holyhead: 3.9 miles

This modern brasserie has fine views over the bay and isle extending to Snowdonia in clear weather. The lengthy menu has many local fish and meat dishes such as smoked haddock fishcakes, crab frittata and Anglesey mussels, fillet of beef with Anglesey oysters and rump of lamb with wild mushrooms. Some simpler lunch specials include sandwiches served on ciabatta and focaccia, and Sunday lunch offers a selection of roasts. Locally made ice cream and tart au citron are among a wide list of puddings.

Personal favourite
• Seared bass fillet on seafood risotto
• Rump of lamb with wild mushrooms

5. Boathouse Bistro

Newry Beach, Holyhead,
Anglesey LL65 1YF
Tel: 01407 762094
Fax: 01407 764898
www.boathouse-hotel.co.uk

From Holyhead: 4.5 miles

The mustard coloured hotel houses a popular bistro that extends into a conservatory overlooking the bay. It serves a range of bar snacks that include lasagne, steak pies, curries and home cooked ham, plus a daily specials board. Local fishermen bring in their catch that regularly includes bass, crab and lobster for which prices are very reasonable. Other daily specialities might be Thai style fish cakes, braised lamb hock, a vegetarian dish and a few steaks. They take pride in their wine list and have a wine club in the hotel.

Personal favourite
• Locally caught lobster
• Pork fillet in honey and mustard sauce

Llanymynech

Llandrillo

1. Seeds
5 Penbryn Cottages,
Llanfyllin, Powys SY22 5AP
Tel: 01691 648604

From Llanymynech: 10.5 miles

This little restaurant in the market town projects on one thing – enthusiasm. It comes straight from the chef/proprietor and his wife whom enjoy food and wine so much themselves they wish to share the experience. The fabulous wine list possibly overshadows the menu. This smart end of terrace red brick and slate house is a good find in this sparsely populated area and has a loyal following from those who share their passion. Mediterranean influences on prime Welsh ingredients make a big impact on diners.

Personal favourite
• Fried lambs' kidneys with grain mustard
• Panoche of cod, salmon, bream and monkfish

2. Tyddyn Llan
Llandrillo, Nr Corwen,
Denbighshire LL21 0ST
Tel: 01490 440264
Fax: 01490 440414
E: tyddynllan@compuserve.com
www.tyddynllan.co.uk

From Llanymynech: 33.3 miles

It is certainly worth the drive over the Berwyn mountains to experience the cuisine and hospitality at the most sophisticated restaurant with rooms in Wales. The modern Welsh cuisine and fairly priced extensive wine list offer something rare. Experience delights such as fresh scallops, bass, turbot, lobster, grouse, partridge, local lamb and beef cooked with amazing precision and flare. The tastiest desserts and a British cheese board make an equal impact to finish, as does the outstanding wine list.

Personal favourite
• Seared scallops with vegetable relish and rocket
• Roast young grouse with bread sauce

3. The West Arms and The Hand Hotel
Llanarmon Dyffryn Ceiriog,
Nr Llangollen, Wrexham LL20 7LD
Tel: 01691 600665 (West Arms)
E: gowestarms@aol.com
www.thewestarms.co.uk
Tel: 01691 600666 (Hand Hotel)
E: reception@thehandhotel.co.uk
www.thehandhotel.co.uk
From Llanymynech: 16 miles

At the foot of the Berwyn Mountains there are two fine hostelries, the Hand Hotel and the West Arms, both renowned for their country cuisine. The latter dates from 1670 and has original features such a huge inglenook in original condition. The dining room exudes ambience and true rural cuisine with all modern sophistications. Expect finest Berwyn lamb, pheasant from the local shoot and fish from Conwy. The Hand has a bar and dining room menu with prime Welsh meats, Ceiriog Valley trout local and organic vegetables competently cooked and presented. A very worthwhile drive.

Personal favourite
• West Arms: Char grilled smoked chicken, leeks, bacon and avocado
• Hand: Braised lamb shank in Guinness and mint

The West Arms   Lake Vyrnwy   Seeds

4. Stumble Inn
Bwlch-y-Cibau, Llanfyllin,
Powys SY22 5LL
Tel: 01691 648860
Fax: 01691 648955

From Llanymynech: 9 miles

This stone built country pub in the tiny village attracts regulars from a wide swathe of the local countryside. The enthusiastic young team cook a wide range of dishes from across the globe. Chicken Kiev is alongside Cajun, Mexican fajhitas and their famous range of curries taking in Madras, korma and jalfrezi. There's also a range of steaks served plain or with creamy sauces and old stalwarts such as boeuf bourguignon. It's very well priced including a few wines and decent ales.

Personal favourite
- Garlic mushrooms
- Thai seafood dim sum with chilli dip

5. Lake Vyrnwy Hotel
Llanwddyn, Nr Welshpool,
Powys SY10 0LY
Tel: 01691 870692
Fax: 01691 870259
E: res@lakevyrnwy.com
www.lakevyrnwy.com

From Llanymynech: 20.2 miles

This fine Victorian Hotel has spectacular views over the reservoir. Food is served in a large sporting bar and country house cuisine in the dining room taking advantage of the view. The menu is international with prime ingredients including turbot, red mullet, game from their own shoot and lamb and beef from their own farm land. Some cooking is complex with a few plainer dishes, including traditional Sunday lunch. Welsh cheeses and an extensive wine list give plenty of choice.

Personal favourite
- Pot roasted pork cutlet on sage mash and calvados jus
- Lime scented pannacotta with peppered strawberries

Machynys

Swansea Marina

Llanddarog
3

1
◄ Machynys

2
Reynoldston

Swansea
4 5

1. Fairyhill Bar and Brasserie

Nicklaus Avenue,
Machynys, Llanelli,
Carmarthenshire SA15 2DG
Tel: 01554 744994
www.fairyhill.net

This separate enterprise within the clubhouse occupies the first floor and hence has magnificent views over the course, the Bury Estuary and Gower Peninsula. Elegant and modern the food is in keeping with surroundings. There's a comfortable lounge area, restaurant and terrace, all for relaxed dining. Snacks are taken in lounge, the menu extending to modern brasserie food. Local specialities include cockles and laverbread, lamb cutlets, Welsh Black Tbone, Joe's ice cream and Welsh cheeses. Cooking and service is highly competent.

Personal favourite
- Beetroot salad with crisp Carmarthen ham
- Aged rump of Welsh Black, pepper sauce

2. Fairyhill Country Hotel

Reynoldston, Gower SA3 1BS
Tel: 01792 390139
E: admin@fairyhill.net
www.fairyhill.net

From Machynys: 16.1 miles

This elegant Georgian house is set in 24 acres of parkland. It serves modern Welsh cuisine par excellence using as much produce from Gower as possible. Bass, crab and lobsters come from local fishermen; salt marsh lamb is from Penclawdd along with fresh cockles, mussels and laverbread. Everything is seasonally fresh including wild mushrooms and game. It's grand cuisine style in the informal ambience of the hotel dining rooms. The wine list has numerous wonderful bottles at fair prices.

Personal favourite
- Seared scallops, cauliflower puree, champagne and orange sauce
- Roast pheasant, celeriac mash, fricassee of girolles, game jus

3. The Butchers Arms

Llanddarog,
Carmarthenshire
SA32 8NS
Tel: 01267 275330
Fax: 01267 275370
www.butchersofllanddarog.co.uk

From Machynys: 17.8 miles

This is a truly welcoming pub with generous portions of food at fair prices. The whitewashed farm style pub has many internal areas plus tables for al fresco dining in the summer. The lengthy menu offers plenty of roasts and grills, with salads and sizzling platters. Their legendary mixed grill is a challenge to most hearty eaters. A short wine list is complemented by a wide range of ales including local Felinfoel from Llanelli.

Personal favourite
- Sizzling platter of garlic prawns
- Welsh Black rump steak

The Butchers Arms   Millennium Coastal Park   Fairyhill Country Hotel

4. Didier and Stephanie
56 St Helen's Road,
Swansea SA1 4BE
Tel: 01792 655603
Fax: 01792 470563

From Machynys: 12.2 miles

A small neat restaurant with pine furnishings has a truly Gallic charm that flows through the food and service. It is true regional French cooking with most influence from Burgundy. Most produce is bought from Swansea Market and local cockles and laverbread are given a French treatment, along with sewin, bass and other seasonally fresh fish. Cooking skill extends to slow cooked casseroles in true bourgeois style, to conciseness with fish and shellfish and well judged sauces. French wines come at very competitive prices.

Personal favourite
• Confit of duck leg with puy lentils
• Pistachio crème brulee

5. La Braseria
28 Wind Street,
Swansea SA1 1DZ
Tel: 01792 469683
www.labraseria.com

From Machynys: 12.3 miles

This large restaurant has the theme of a Spanish bodega. Long chill counters are piled with the fare that takes in juicy steaks and other meats and a wide selection of fish in the upstairs area. Cooking is mainly on the chargrill, in the fryer or oven, and results speak for themselves. Steaks are cooked perfectly to request, fresh fish is very reliable and the accompaniments of salad, jacket potatoes and chips please all. There's a vast cellar of fairly priced wine, particularly from Rioja.

Personal favourite
• Bass Galician style baked in sea salt
• Char grilled rump steak

Nefyn

View south to Nefyn

Nefyn
Pwllheli
Criccieth
Aberdaron
Abersoch
1
5
2
3 4

1. Plas Bodegroes

Nefyn Road, Pwllheli,
Gwynedd LL53 5TH
Tel: 01758 612363
Fax: 01758 701247
www.bodegroes.co.uk

Closed: Dec – Feb
From Nefyn: 5.1 miles

This beautiful Georgian mansion surrounded by lawns is one of the finest restaurants in Wales and holds a Michelin Star. The discreet modern dining room has an air of calm and a perfect setting for the style of cuisine. Everything is locally sourced and cooking reaches great heights in well judged dishes. Seafood excels and creativity extends to treatment with fish, meat and desserts alike. The extensive wine list is a statement of dedication to quality and the service is smooth and efficient.

Personal favourite
• Scallops in Carmarthen Ham
• Rack of salt marsh lamb

2. Porth Tocyn Hotel

Bwlch Tocyn, Abersoch,
Gwynedd LL53 7BU
Tel: 01758 713303
Fax: 01758 713538
E: bookings@porthtocyn.fsnet.co.uk
www.porth-tocyn-hotel.co.uk

Closed: Nov – March
From Nefyn: 14.3 miles

This cliff top hotel has views extending over Cardigan Bay to Snowdonia. The traditional dining room with parquet floor and oak furniture has a clubby feel, as many regulars know the owners well. It has been Good Food Guide listed for forty years and still serves accomplished cuisine cooked by the family and their chefs. Local fish are cooked with style and meat dishes include venison, pheasant, local pork, lamb and Welsh Black beef. The help yourself cheese table completes the ambience. Wines are well priced.

Personal favourite
• Seared grey mullet with tomato fondue, anchovy and black olive
• Feuillete of braised wild rabbit with seared loin with liquorice sauce

3. Ship Inn

Aberdaron, Gwynedd LL53 8BE
Tel: 01758 760204
www.theshiphotelaberdaron.co.uk

From Nefyn: 13.7 miles

This very popular seaside resort at the end of the Llyn Peninsula has its own fishing fleet that lands fresh lobster, crabs and prime fish to this traditional inn in the small town centre. Though the emphasis is obviously seafood their treatment of Welsh lamb and beef is equally skilled. Sample their grilled lobster, take up a cracker and pick and extract every succulent morcel. The small dining room does get very busy and some delays are unavoidable, but the wait worthwhile.

Personal favourite
• Grilled lobster with garlic beurre blanc
• Dressed Aberdaron crab

Plas Bodegroes | Salt marsh lamb | Ship Inn

4. Penbryn Bach
Uwchmynydd, Aberdaron,
Gwynedd LL53 8BY
T: 01758 760216

Closed: Nov – March
From Nefyn: 15.2 miles

This is certainly out of the way on the road from Aberdaron to Bardsey. Freshest crab and locally landed fish are the attraction. There are two dining areas and a cosy lounge with wood burning stoves for comfort in poor weather. Most fish is simply cooked to display its freshness, and a few more elaborate dishes such as salmon en croute give variety as do a few steak and vegetarian dishes. The value for money is unquestionable and the few wines are extremely well priced.

Personal favourite
• Ginger crab cakes
• Moules mariniere

5. Granvilles
28 High Street, Criccieth,
Gwynedd LL52 0BT
Tel: 01766 522506

Closed: Dec – Feb
From Nefyn: 13 miles

The brightly coloured shop frontage is the stage door for a coffee shop during the day and a more serious restaurant in the evening. The simply decorated room extends to a garden overlooking the bay. Day offerings include baked potatoes, paninis and salads plus a few daily specials; in the night items such as moules mariniere, home made soups, braised dishes such as lamb shank and roasts including duck and chicken. Capable cooking and fair prices make it an enjoyable venue.

Personal favourite
• Tomato and basil soup
• Gressingham duck with grapefruit and redcurrant sauce

Pyle & Kenfig

Wales Millennium Centre

1. Armless Dragon

97-99 Wyeverne Road,
Cathays, Cardiff CF24 4BG
Tel: 029 2038 2357
Fax: 029 2038 2055
www.thearmlessdragon.co.uk

From Pyle & Kenfig: 27.5miles

This small restaurant delivers far more than one would expect from its aspect and location. Though understated it is the gem of the culinary scene in Cardiff. The menu has a host of carefully sourced foods from around Wales from finest free range chickens, to wild game, organic meats, trawler landed fish and crustaceans, farmhouse butter and artisan cheeses. These are cooked with great skill and precision to bring out their best qualities, with brilliant desserts rounding the meal to perfection.

Personal favourite
- Seared breast and slow cooked leg of mature pheasant
- Cinnamon bread and butter pudding

2. Old Post Office

Greenwood Lane,
St Fagans, Cardiff CF5 6EL
Tel: 029 2056 5400
Fax: 029 2056 3400

From Pyle & Kenfig: 25 miles

This ultra modern minimalist designed contemporary restaurant is close to the Museum of Welsh Life at St Fagans. The cuisine is similarly up to date and is a subtle mix of traditional cooking with Italian influences showing through. Ingredients are first class sourced from around Wales including Penllyn venison, cockles and laverbread. Confident cooking produces strident dishes. Smoked venison with walnut chutney, rabbit casserole with mustard, and risotto of artichokes are typical. Prices are very fair for the quality.

Personal favourite
- Classic Italian fish casserole
- Roasted squash tagliatelli with sage and walnut dressing

3. La Marina

Custom House, Penarth Marina,
Cardiff Bay, Cardiff CF64 1TT
Tel: 029 2070 5544
Fax: 029 2070 7337

From Pyle & Kenfig: 29.7 miles

The imposing former Customs House on Penarth Marina is the up-dated Spanish bodega style with contemporary décor and a first floor fine dining restaurant La Marina. The large bar always has Champagne at bargain prices. The chill counters are stacked with tempting meat, seafood and salads to be cooked in the time honoured style. Concise cooking of the same ingredients with careful saucing and garnishes marks the style of La Marina. There is a vast choice of wines at every conceivable level.

Personal favourite
- Lobster grilled with garlic butter
- Rump of venison with red cabbage

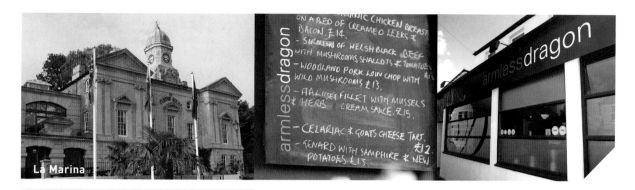

La Marina

4. Egerton Grey
Porthkerry, Barry,
Vale of Glamorgan CF62 3BZ
Tel: 01446 711666
Fax: 01446 711690
E: info@egertongrey.co.uk
www.egertongrey.co.uk

From Pyle & Kenfig: 31 miles

This splendid Victorian country house is packed with antiques. Dinner is taken in the Cuban teak panelled former billiard room. Menus have plenty of Welsh specialities including Pembroke crab and Welsh Black beef. There are simpler dishes for lighter dining with first rate fish and chips and sausage and mash. Crab risotto with ginger and spring onion, rack of lamb with root vegetables, and bass with sauce vierge mark the more serious dishes. Sunday lunch offers a choice of several roasts and fish.

Personal favourite
• Corn fed chicken breast, artichoke mash, field mushroom sauce
• White chocolate and raspberry cheesecake

Royal Porthcawl

Rest Bay, Porthcawl

1. Court Colman
Pen-y-Fai, Bridgend CF31 4NG
Tel: 01656 720212
Fax: 01656 724544
E: experience@court-colman-manor.com
www.court-colman-manor.com

From Royal Porthcawl: 5.3 miles

This huge edifice of a Victorian Mansion seems an unlikely venue for a first class Indian restaurant that also combines with a modern brasserie. The Bhagotra Brasserie is spacious and plush, with an open kitchen where the chefs can be seen making vibrantly tasty spicy meat, poultry and fish dishes of all descriptions. They might also be char grilling steaks and Dover sole, or baking bass in sea salt. The result is quite harmonious and a very entertaining evening.

Personal favourite
• Tandoori local farm lamb
• Grilled Dover sole

2. Great House
The Great House Hotel & Leicester's Restaurant, High Street, Laleston, Bridgend CF32 0HP
Tel: 01656 657644
Fax: 01656 668892
E: enquiries@great-house-laleston.co.uk
www.great-house-laleston.co.uk

From Royal Porthcawl: 3.5 miles

This is certainly a grand venue with the flamboyant Leicester's Restaurant. The décor is in keeping with a manor house, and the food colourful and presented with aplomb. The menu has plenty of local Welsh foods, including Black beef and lamb and a range of fish. The cooking puts together some interesting combinations and these are well received. The dessert trolley is most tempting with liqueur laced specialities and a selection of Welsh farmhouse cheeses.

Personal favourite
• Organic salmon, seared foie gras, braised puy lentils, coriander nage
• Rump of lamb with garlic mash, white bean fricassee

3. Coed y Mwstwr
Coychurch, Bridgend CF35 6AF
Tel: 01656 860621
Fax: 01656 863122
E: enquiries@coed-y-mwstwr.com
www.coed-y-mwstwr.com

From Royal Porthcawl: 8.5 miles

This red brick Victorian Manor has been a restaurant and hotel for forty years. It has always been known for its fine table and it's in keeping with the style of the house. Presentations are grand and many dishes quite complex. The ingredients are well sourced and novel ideas such as black pudding fritters with herb butter and smoked chicken liver parfait are very tasty and different. Game in season, very reliable Welsh beef and correctly cooked salmon are always popular. Service is very attentive and gives a relaxing air.

Personal favourite
• Peppered fillet of beef with honey mustard
• Loin of pork with red cabbage

Coed y Mwstwr | Organic salmon | Le Gallois

4. El Prado
High Street, Laleston,
Bridgend CF32 0LD
Tel: 01656 649972

From Royal Porthcawl: 3.5 miles

A Spanish brasserie with a similar style to others in Cardiff and Swansea this certainly packs people in. The ever popular selection of steaks, lamb and other meats, plus the fish counter gives a wide choice to be char grilled on la parilla, roast or deep fried as appropriate. Help yourself salads, bread, water and wine can push the cost up, but it is the most popular place in the area.

Personal favourite
• Crisp fried monkfish
• Sirloin steak with pepper sauce

5. Le Gallois
6 –10 Romilly Crescent,
Canton, Cardiff CF11 9NR
Tel: 029 20341264
Fax: 029 20237911
E: info@legallois-ycymro.com
www.legallois-ycymro.com

From Royal Porthcawl: 27.5 miles

This restaurant has been popular for decades and as Le Gallois it is one of the most popular in Cardiff and worthy of the drive. Elegant modern décor is the setting for fine modern Welsh/French cuisine. A high degree of technical flair transforms traditional dishes into something intelligently innovative. The accompaniments and trimmings are spot on. Mastery with fish includes olive crusted bass. Slow cooked lamb comes with chestnut mash. This extends to desserts, home made ices and patisserie. A comprehensive wine list matches the style.

Personal favourite
• Ox tail terrine with horseradish, dandelion salad
• Hot chocolate fondant with pistachio ice cream

Royal St David's

Harlech castle

Porthmadog
5 4 Portmeirion
1 3
Harlech

2 Barmouth

1. Castle Cottage

Y Llech, Harlech, Gwynedd LL46 2YL
Tel: 01766 780479
Fax: 01766 780479
www.castlecottageharlech.co.uk

From Royal St David's: 0.4 miles

This seventeenth century coaching house is tucked behind the walls of the mighty Harlech Castle. Smart modern décor blends well in the lounges and dining room. Cooking is assertive and accomplished from carefully sourced ingredients. The menu features Rhydlewis smoked salmon, Barmouth lobster, Conwy mussels and sole, local lamb and Welsh Black beef, with house specials of porchetta, mushroom strudel, and crisp lamb pancakes. Puddings hit the balance between elegance and extravagance. A great wine list is good value.

Personal favourite
- Rack of lamb on herb crust with garlic potatoes
- Chocolate, Tia Maria and cappuccino mousse

2. Bae Abermaw

Panorama Road, Barmouth,
Gwynedd LL42 1DQ
Tel: 01341 280550
Fax: 01341 280346
E: enquiries@baeabermaw.com
www.baeabermaw.com

From Royal St David's: 11 miles

This traditional stone mansion is in the aptly named Panorama Road. Elegant modern furnishings sit well in the minimalist décor with the backdrop of Cardigan Bay. The black and white restaurant is the setting for a host of local produce plus inspired vegetarian dishes. Pantysgawn goats' cheese soufflé with roasted Mediterranean vegetables and tagliatelle with girolles join sole, bass, beef, duck and lamb on a menu that draws from local suppliers. A big effort goes into the inspired dessert selection

Personal favourite
- Smoked haddock Welsh rarebit on tomato salad
- Fillet of Welsh Black with caramelised shallots

3. Maes y Neuadd, Talsarnau

Talsarnau, Harlech, Gwynedd LL47 6YA
Tel: 01766 780200
Fax: 01766 780211
E: maes@neuadd.com
www.neuadd.com

From Royal St David's: 4.7 miles

The mansion in the meadows is on a wooded hillside and has views to Snowdonia and the Llyn Peninsula. It is renowned for fine cuisine that comes in a four course dinner featuring local fish such as sewin, bass, gurnard and red mullet, plus Snowdonia lamb, farm pork and duck. Puddings make a statement with aplomb. Lunches include some more hearty dishes, perhaps braised ox tail, confit of duck and meatballs, and delicious crab cakes, goujons of fish and smoked salmon. A snack menu is served all afternoon.

Personal favourite
- Cutlet of pork with garden Brussels and potato rosti
- Poached pear in red wine, dark chocolate sauce

Maes y Neuadd

Welsh Black beef

4. Portmeirion and Castell Deudraeth

Portmeirion, Gwynedd LL48 6ET
Tel: 01766 770000
Fax: 01766 771331
E: enquiries@portmeirion-village.com
www.portmeirion-village.com

From Royal St David's: 8.8 miles

This is the most enchanting place in Wales. The hotel's dining room has the feel of an ocean liner and overlooks the Traeth Estuary. Much of the food is from the Llyn and Snowdonia, served in grand cuisine style. Fresh fish features regularly including bass, salmon, sewin, sole and lobster. Traeth salt marsh lamb and local game in season make an interesting menu. Castell Deudraeth in the same grounds has been superbly refurbished and makes a less formal alternative at more everyday prices.

Personal favourite
- Llyn crab thermidor
- Breast of duck with sweet and sour cabbage

5. Yr Hen Fecws

16 Lombard Street, Porthmadog,
Gwynedd LL49 9AP
Tel: 01766 514625
Fax: 01766 514865
E: enquiries@henfecws.com
www.henfecws.com

From Royal St David's: 9.6 miles

An old bakehouse in a row of cottages on the quay, this little restaurant with rooms serves truly homely food. It's very cosy and informal with chapel pews and Welsh slate table mats. The menu is traditional, the cooking straightforward and service very friendly. Welsh lamb shank braised with wild mushrooms, crisp roast duck and chargrilled steaks are all presented nicely and from prime ingredients. Comfort puddings are particularly homely and always popular. Wines come at bargain prices.

Personal favourite
- Chicken liver and Cointreau pate
- Braised lamb shank with wild mushrooms

Southerndown

1. Frolics

Beach Road, Southerndown,
Vale of Glamorgan CF32 0RP
Tel: 01656 880127

From Southerndown: 0.2 miles

This oasis on the cliffs of Southerndown has established a fine reputation for highly creative cuisine. The chef driven business seeks out the finest seasonal ingredients and the menu changes accordingly. The use of fish landed in Wales, and meat reared on Welsh farms combined with some modish ingredients delivers a fine repertoire of dishes. Novel combinations and original creations such as mussels, lime and piri piri risotto, and Tenby lobster pastries with thermidor sauce are inspiring. To finish Welsh cheese or patisserie is first rate.

Personal favourite
- Pan seared bass with scallop, pancetta, claret sauce
- 5 hour confit of belly pork, roast langoustine, leek and mushroom sauce

2. Plough and Harrow

Monknash, Nr Cowbridge,
Vale of Glamorgan CF71 7QQ
Tel: 01656 890209
E: info@theploughmonknash.com
www.theploughmonknash.com

From Southerndown: 4.7 miles

This traditional pub is steeped in history. It has been long renowned for serving real ales and a fine table. The daytime menu has a host of hearty dishes including traditional faggots, steak and Guinness pie, Glamorgan sausages, soup and baguettes. Evenings the choice is wider with a regularly changing menu. This offers items such as mussels, smoked duck, tiger prawns, garlic mushrooms, with several fish and meaty dishes to follow. It's excellent value and a truly entertaining place for a good evening.

Personal favourite
- Lobster bisque
- Rack of lamb with rosemary and redcurrant sauce

3. Huddarts

69 High Street, Cowbridge,
Vale of Glamorgan CF71 7AF
Tel: 01446 774645
Fax: 01446 772215

From Southerndown: 9.3 miles

This restaurant in the fashionable town of Cowbridge offers a very credible range of dishes. These are described in great detail down to every ingredient. It's set in a town house in the high street run by a couple who oversee everything. Dishes include some top Welsh ingredients, including Welsh Black beef and Penllyne lamb, plus Penclawdd cockles, laverbread and black pudding. In season prime fish as turbot comes perfectly with beurre blanc, and game, including partridge is served traditionally. Wines are very fairly priced.

Personal favourite
- Lobster bisque
- Saddle of lamb with redcurrant jus

Vale Hotel

Plough and Harrow

4. Vale Hotel
Hensol Park, Hensol,
Vale of Glamorgan CF72 8JY
Tel: 01443 667800
Fax: 01443 667801
E: reservations@vale-hotel.com
www.vale-hotel.com

From Southerndown: 16 miles

This large modern hotel, spa and golf complex has two restaurants, the more formal Lakes and the Mediterranean style La Cucina, both in the wonderful setting of Hensol Park. Med style food includes pizza and pasta plus grills and a few fish and other meat dishes served lunch and dinner. More formal evenings can be enjoyed at Lakes. Here the menu has a concise selection of quality Welsh meat in modern presentations, preceded by perhaps scallops, smoked duck breast or terrine on a daily changing menu.

Personal favourite
• Ricotta stuffed breast of chicken in Carmarthen ham
• Rack of Welsh lamb with olive and capers and fondant potatoes

5. Le Monde, Brasserie, Champers
62 St Mary Street, Cardiff CF10 1FE
Tel: 029 2038 7376
Fax: 029 2066 8092
E: mail@le-monde-co.uk
www.le-monde.co.uk

From Southerndown: 24.5 miles

This vast restaurant complex close to the Millennium Stadium in Cardiff was the original Spanish bodega style that began in Champers. With close on a thousand seats it's an impressive operation. Counters of steak, various meats, a groaning selection of fish including oysters are presented for self selection. It's then cooked on the char grill, perhaps fish is deep fried or baked Galician style. Spanish and French wines plus Champagne come at competitive prices. The place is buzzing and always good fun.

Personal favourite
• Deep fried hake with tartare sauce
• Sirloin steak with jacket potato and mixed salad

Tenby

1. Old Kings Arms
13 Main Street, Pembroke,
Pembrokeshire SA71 4JS
Tel: 01646 683611
Fax: 01646 682335
E: info@oldkingsarmshotel.co.uk
www.oldkingsarmshotel.co.uk

From Tenby: 11.3 miles

This well known local in Pembroke has a popular bar and lounge and a traditional restaurant. It has been serving good food in the bar and restaurant for decades and still keeps up to date with food style and gives due attention to quality ingredients. Superb fresh fish from Milford includes sole, sewin, plaice, crab and lobster. Pembrokeshire organic meat such as Welsh Black beef and salt marsh lamb is cooked with precision. It is informal and relaxing, with a particularly tempting wine list at bargain prices.

Personal favourite
• Wheeler's King Prawns in garlic butter
• Slow roasted leg of duck on juniper cabbage

2. St Brides Spa Hotel
Saundersfoot, Pemrokeshire,
SA69 9NH
Tel: 01834 8121304
Fax: 01834 811766
E: reservations@stbridesspahotel.com
www.stbridesspahotel.com

From Tenby: 2.6 miles

This magnificently refurbished traditional hotel has wonderful vistas over the sandy bay and rocky coastline. The restaurant is elegant, modern and spacious with contemporary artwork. The menu is similarly in vogue and items such as smoked chicken, wild mushrooms, mozzarella, red snapper, Dover sole, cornfed chicken, calves liver and fillet steak cater for a wide clientele. The Gallery bar has mouth watering lighter dishes including eggs Benedict and fresh mussels at very reasonable prices. A large terrace is perfect for summer dining.

Personal favourite
• Haddock fillet on black pudding mash with pea puree
• Local venison, fondant potatoes, root vegetable jus

3. Cors
Newbridge Road, Laugharne,
Carmarthenshire SA33 4SH
Tel: 01994 427219
www.the-cors.co.uk

From Tenby: 21 miles

This elegant yet slightly faded Victorian gentleman's residence has a very homely feel. It has a truly splendid garden tended by the proprietor who also cooks with flare. The menu is sensibly limited but everything will be the freshest. Local salt marsh lamb from Dylan Thomas' heron priested estuary, or sewin from the Taf, perhaps Welsh Black beef and Pembroke scallops make a salivating menu with delicious fresh vegetables. Pre and post drinks in the bar complete the relaxing evening.

Personal favourite
• Sewin with beurre blanc sauce
• Welsh Black fillet with green peppercorns and red wine sauce

Old Point House

THE OLD KINGS ARMS HOTEL — DIEU ET MON DROIT

Lobster salad

4. Old Point House

Angle, Nr, Pembroke,
Pembrokeshire SA71 5AS
Tel: 01646 641205

From Tenby: 18.3 miles

A cottage pub on the Pembrokeshire coastal path is on the west of the Premier County. It is stacked with nautical artefacts and charts and has a homely dining room. The proprietors own a trawler and hence fresh fish is superb. Expect line caught mackerel and bass, freshest lobster and crab and what ever might come up in the net. Eat in the bar for a quick snack of fresh prawn sandwiches, home made terrines and hearty desserts. Great real ale and a few wines are reasonable.

Personal favourite
• Cod fillet with leeks and basil cream
• Lobster salad

5. Hurst House

East Marsh, Laugharne,
Carmarthenshire SA33 4RS
Tel: 01994 427417
Fax: 01994 427730
www.hurst-house.co.uk

From Tenby: 20 miles

A former manor farm on the edge of the Laugharne salt marsh is now a boutique hotel with its own spa. Stunning modern décor is carefully blended into the traditional features. Flamboyant food is served in the restaurant with a range of simple snacks from burgers upwards in the spacious lounge bar. Lots of sauces and garnishes adorn plates, but it's generally tasty and carefully cooked. Local lamb and seafood feature alongside smoked duck breast and mushroom ravioli. It's a truly enjoyable place to stay.

Personal favourite
• Fillet of bass on saffron potatoes
• Cannon of lamb with watercress sauce

Golf clubs in Wales

A

Aberdare Golf Club, Abernant, Aberdare
CF44 0RY 01685 872797
www.aberdaregolfclub.co.uk

Aberdovey Golf Club, Aberdovey LL35 0RT
01654 767493
www.aberdoveygolf.co.uk

Abergele Golf Club, Tan-y-Goppa Road,
Abergele LL22 8DS 01745 824034
www.abergelegolfclub.co.uk

Abersoch Golf Club, Golf Road Abersoch,
Pwllheli LL53 7EY 01758 712636
www.abersochgolf.co.uk

Aberystwyth Golf Club, Brynymor Road,
Aberystwyth, Ceredigion SY23 2HY
01970 615104
www.aberystwythgolfclub.com

Alice Springs Golf Club, Bettws Newydd, Usk
NP15 1JY 01873 880708
www.alicespringsgolfclub.co.uk

Allt-y-Graban Golf Club, Alltygraban Road,
Pontlliw Swansea SA4 1DT 01792 885757

Anglesey Golf Club, Station Road, Rhosneigr
LL64 5QX 01407 811202
www.angleseygolfclub.co.uk

Ashburnham Golf Club, Cliff Terrace,
Burry Port SA16 0HN 01554 832269
www.ashburnhamgolfclub.co.uk

B

Bala (Penlan) Golf Club, Penlan, Y Bala
LL23 7YQ 01678 520359

Bargoed Golf Club, Heolddu, Bargoed
CF81 9GF 01443 830143

Baron Hill Golf Club, Beaumaris LL58 8YW
01248 810231
www.baronhill.co.uk

Betws-y-Coed Golf Club, Old Church Road,
Betws-y-coed LL24 0AL 01690 710556
www.golf-betws-y-coed.co.uk

Blackwood Golf Club, Cwmgelli, Blackwood
NP12 1BR 01495 222121

Borth & Ynyslas Golf Club, Borth SY24 5JS
01970 871202
www.borthgolf.co.uk

Brecon Golf Club, Newton Park, Llanfaes,
Brecon LD3 8PA 01874 622004

Bridgend Golf Complex, Golden Mile,
Corntown, Bridgend CF35 5AS 01656 647926
www.bridgendgolf.co.uk

Bryn Meadows Golf Club, Maesycwmmer,
Nr Ystrad Mynach, Caerphilly CF82 7SN
01495 225590
www.brynmeadows.co.uk

Bryn Morfydd Golf Club, Llanrhaeadr,
Denbigh LL16 4NP 01745 890280

Brynhill Golf Club, Port Road, Barry CF62 8PN
01446 720277
www.brynhillgolfclub.co.uk

Builth Wells Golf Club, The Clubhouse,
Golf Club Road, Builth Wells LD32 3NF
01982 553296
www.builthwellsgolf.co.uk

Bull Bay Golf Club, Bull Bay Road, Amlwch
LL68 9RY 01407 830960
www.bullbaygc.co.uk

C

Caerleon Golf Club, Broadway, Caerleon,
Newport NP18 1AY 01633 420342

Caernarfon Golf Club, Aberforeshire,
Llanfaglan, Caernarfon LL54 5RP
01286 673783

Caerphilly Golf Club, Pencapel, Mountain
Road, Caerphilly CF83 1HJ 02920 863441
www.caerphillygolfclub.com

Cardiff Golf Club, Sherborne Avenue, Cyncoed,
Cardiff CF23 6SJ 02920 753320
www.cardiffgc.co.uk

Cardigan Golf Club, Gwbert-on-Sea, Cardigan
SA43 1PR 01239 621775
www.cardigangolf.co.uk

Carmarthen Golf Club, Blaenycoed Road,
Carmarthen SA33 6EH 01267 281588
www.carmarthengolfclub.com

Castell Heights Golf Club, Blaengwynlais,
Caerphilly CF8 1NG 02920 886666
www.golfclub.co.uk

Celtic Manor Resort, Coldra Woods, Newport
NP18 1HQ 01633 413000
www.celtic-manor.com

Chirk Golf Club, Chirk, Wrexham LL14 5AD
01691 774407
www.jackbarker.com

Cilgwyn Golf Club, Llangybi, Lampeter
SA48 8NN 01570 493286

Clay's Golf Centre, Bryn Estyn Road,
Llan-y-Pwll, Wrexham LL13 9UB
01978 661406
www.claysgolf.co.uk

Clyne Golf Club, 118-120 Owl's Lodge Lane,
Mayals, Swansea SA3 5DP 01792 401989
www.clynegolfclub.com

Coed-y-Mwstwr Golf Club, Coychurch,
Bridgend CF35 6AF 01656 864934
www.coed-y-mwstwr.co.uk

Conwy (Caernarvonshire) Golf Club, Beacons
Way, Morfa Conwy LL32 8ER 01492 592423
www.conwygolfclub.co.uk

Corus Golf Club, The Course, Groes, Margam,
Port Talbot SA13 2NF 01639 871111 (ext. 3368)

Cottrell Park Golf Club, St Nicholas, Cardiff
CF5 6JY 01446 781781
www.golfwithus.com

Cradoc Golf Club, Penoyre Park, Cradoc,
Brecon LD3 9LP 01874 623658
www.cradoc.co.uk

Creigiau Golf Club, Llantwit Road, Creigiau,
Cardiff CF15 9NN 02920 890263
www.creigiaugolf.co.uk

Criccieth Golf Club, Ednyfed Hill, Criccieth
LL52 0PH 01766 522154
www.cricciethgolfclub.co.uk

Cwmrhydneuadd Golf Club, Cwmrhydneuadd,
Plwmp, Llandysul SA44 6HD 01239 654933

D

Dawn til Dusk Golf Club, Rosemarket, Milford
Haven SA73 1JY 01437 890281
www.dawntilldusk.co.uk

Denbigh Golf Club, Henllan Road, Denbigh
LL16 5AA 01745 816669
www.denbighgolfclub.co.uk

Derllys Golf Club, Llysonnen Road,
Carmarthen SA33 5DT 01267 211575
www.derllyscourtgolfclub.com

Dewstow Golf Club, Caerwent NP26 5AH
01291 430444
www.dewstow.com

Dinas Powys Golf Club, Highwalls Road, Dinas
Powys CF64 4AJ 02920 512727

Dollgellau Golf Club, Pencefn Road, Dolgellau
LL40 2ES 01341 422603
www.dolgellaugolfclub.com

E

Earlswood Golf Club, Jersey Marine, Neath
SA10 6JP 01792 321578

F

Fairwood Park Golf Club, Blackhills Lane,
Upper Killay Swansea SA2 7JN 01792 297849
/ 01792 299194 www.fairwoodpark.com

Ffestiniog Golf Club, Y Cefn, Ffestiniog
01766 762637
www.ffestinioggolf.org

Flint Golf Club, Cornist Park, Flint CH6 5HJ
01352 732327
www.flintgolfclub.netfirms.com

G

Garnant Park Golf Club, Dinefwr Road,
Garnant, Ammanford SA18 1NP 01269 823365
www.parcgarnantgolf.co.uk

Glamorganshire Golf Club, Lavernock Road,
Penarth CF64 5UP 029 20701185
www.glamorganshiregolfclub.co.uk

Glyn Abbey Golf Club, Trimsarn SA17 4LB
01554 810278
www.glynabbey.co.uk

Glynhir Golf Club, Glynhir Road, Llandybie,
Ammanford SA18 2TF 01269 850472
www.glynhirgolfclub.co.uk

Glynneath Golf Club, Penygraig,
Pontneathvaughan, Glynneath SA11 5UH
01639 720452
www.glynneathgolfclub.co.uk

Gower Golf Course, Cefn Goleu, Three
Crosses, Swansea SA4 3HS 01792 872480
www.gowergolf.co.uk

Gowerton Golf Range, Victoria Road, Gowerton, Swansea SA4 3AB 01792 875188

Greenmeadow Golf Club, Treherbert Road, Croesyceiliog, Cwmbran NP44 2BZ
01633 862626
www.greenmeadowgolf.com

Grove Golf Club, South Cornelly, Nr Porthcawl, Bridgend CF33 4RP
01656 788771 www.grovegolf.com

H

Haverfordwest Golf Club, Arnoldsdown, Haverfordwest SA61 2XQ 01437 764523
www.haverfordwestgolfclub.co.uk

Hawarden Golf Club, Groomsdale Lane, Hawarden CH5 3EH 01244 531447
www.hawardengolfclub.co.uk

Henllys Hall Golf Club, Beaumaris LL58 8HU
01248 811303

Holyhead Golf Club, Lon Garreg Fawr, Trearddur Bay LL65 2YL 01407 763279
www.holyheadgolfclub.co.uk

Holywell Golf Club, Brynford, Holywell CH8 8LQ 01352 713937
www.holywellgolfclub.holywellgc.co.uk

I

INCO Golf Club Clydach, Swansea SA6 5QR
01792 841257

K

Kinsale Golf Club, Llanercymhor, Holywell CH8 9DT 01745 561080

Knighton Golf Club, Ffyrdd Wood, Knighton LD7 1DG 01547 528646
www.knightongolfclub.co.uk

L

Lakeside Golf Club, Water Street, Margam, Port Talbot SA13 2PA 01639 899959
www.lakesidegolf.co.uk

Langland Bay Golf Club, Langland Bay Road, Langland, Swansea SA3 4QR 01792 361721
www.langlandbaygolfclub.com

Llandovery College Golf Course, Llandovery SA20 0EE 01550 723000
www.llandoverycollege.com

Llandrindod Wells Golf Club, The Clubhouse, Llandrindod Wells LD1 5NY 01597 823873
www.lwgc.co.uk

Llandudno (Maesdu) Golf Club, Hospital Road, Llandudno LL30 1HU 01492 876450
www.maesdugolfclub.co.uk

Llandudno North Wales Golf Club, 72 Bryniau Road, West Shore, Llandudno LL30 2DZ
01492 875325
www.northwalesgolfclub.co.uk

Llanfairfechan Golf Club, Llanerch Road, Llanfairfechan LL30 0EB 01248 680144

Llangefni Golf Club, Llangefni LL77 8YQ
01248 722193

Llanishen Golf Club, Heol Hir, Llanishen, Cardiff CF14 9UD 029 2075 5078
www.llanishengc.co.uk

Llantrisant & Pontyclun Golf Club, Off Ely Valley Road, Talbot Green CF72 8AL
01443 222148
www.llantrisantandpontyclungc.co.uk

Llanwern Golf Club, Tennyson Avenue, Llanwern, Newport NP18 2DN 01633 412029
www.llanwerngolfclub.co.uk

Llanymynech Golf Club, Pant, Oswestry SY10 8LB 01691 830983
www.llanymynechgolfclub.co.uk

Llanyrafon Golf Club, Llanfrechfa Way, Cwmbran NP44 8HT 01633 874636

M

Machynlleth Golf Club, Newtown Road, Machynlleth SY20 8UH 01654 702000

Machynys Golf & Country Club, Nicklaus Avenue, Machynys, Llanelli SA15 2DG
01554 744888 www.machynys.com

Maesmawr Golf Club, Mid Wales Golf Centre, Caersws SY17 5SB 01686 668303

Maesteg Golf Club, Mount Pleasant, Neath Road, Maesteg CF34 9PR 01656 734106
www.maesteg-golf.co.uk

Marriott St Pierre Golf, Hotel & Country Club, St Pierre Park, Chepstow NP6 6YA
01291 625261

Milford Haven Golf Club, Woodland Way, Clay Lane, Milford Haven SA73 3RX 01646 697822
www.mhgc.co.uk

Mayfield Golf and Driving Range, Clareston Hill, Freystrop, Haverfordwest SA62 4EU
01437 764300

Merthyr Tydfil Golf Club, Cilsanws Mountain, Cefn Coed, Merthyr Tydfil CF48 2NU
01685 723308

Mold Golf Club, Cilcain Road, Pantymwyn, Mold CH7 5EH 01352 741513
www.moldgolfclub.co.uk

Monmouth Golf Club, Leasbrook Lane, Monmouth NP25 3SN 01600 712212
www.monmouthgolfclub.co.uk

Monmouthshire Golf Club, Llanfoist, Abergavenny NP7 9HE 01873 852606

Morlais Castle Golf Club, Pant, Merthyr Tydfil CF48 2UY 01685 722822

Morriston Golf Club, 160 Clasemount Road, Morriston, Swansea SA6 6AJ 01792 796528
www.morristongolfclub.co.uk

Moss Valley Golf Club, Moss Road, Wrexham LL11 4UR 01978 720518

Mountain Ash Golf Club, The Clubhouse, Cefnpennar, Mountain Ash CF45 4DT
01443 479459
www.mountainashgc.co.uk

Mountain Lakes Golf Club, 20 Ash Walk, Talbot Green CF72 8RE 02920 861128

N

Neath Golf Club, Cadoxton, Neath SA10 8AH
01639 633693
www.neathgolfclub.com

Nefyn & District Golf Club, Lon Golf, Morfa, Nefyn LL53 6DA 01758 720966
www.nefyn-golf-club.com

Newport (Gwent) Golf Club, Great Oak, Rogerstone, Newport NP10 9FX 01633 892643
www.newportgolfclub.org.uk

Newport (Pembs) Golf Club, Newport SA42 0NR 01239 820244

Nine of Clubs Golf Course, Caerwys, Nr Mold CH7 5AQ 07703 558840

Northop Golf Club, Northop, Chester CH7 6WA
01352 840440
www.northopgolf.co.uk

O

Oakdale Golf Club, Llwynon Lane, Oakdale, Blackwood NP2 0NF 01495 220044

Old Colwyn Golf Club, The Clubhouse, Woodland Avenue, Old Colwyn LL29 9NL
01492 515581
www.oldcolwyngolfclub.co.uk

Old Padeswood Golf Club, Station Road, Padeswood, Mold CH7 4JL 01244 547401
www.oldpadeswoodgolfclub.co.uk

Old Rectory Golf Club, Llangattock, Crickhowell NP8 1PH 01873 810373
www.rectoryhotel.co.uk

P

Padeswood & Buckley Golf Club, The Caia, Station Lane, Padeswood CH7 4JD
01244 550537

Palleg Golf Club, Palleg Road, Lower Cwmrwrch, Swansea SA9 2QQ 01639 842193
www.palleg-golf.co.uk

Parc Golf Club, Church Lane, Coedkernew, Newport NP10 8TU 01633 680933
www.parcgolf.co.uk

Penmaenmawr Golf Club, Conwy Old Road, Penmaenmawr LL34 6RD 01492 623330
www.pengolf.co.uk

Pennant Park Golf Club, Whitford, Holywell CH8 9EP 01745 563000
www.pennant-park.co.uk

Pennard Golf Club, 2 Southgate Road, Southgate Swansea SA3 2BT 01792 233131
www.pennardgolfclub.com

Penrhos Golf Club, Llanrhystud SY23 5AY
01974 202999
www.penrhosgolf.co.uk

Penrhyn Golf Complex, Llanddaniel, Gaerwen, LL60 6NP 01248 421150

Peterstone Golf Club, Wentloog, Cardiff CF3 8TN 01633 680009
www.peterstonelakes.com

Plassey Golf Club, Eyton, Wrexham LL13 0SP
01978 780020
www.plasseygolf.com

Pontardawe Golf Club, Cefn Lane,
Pontardawe, Swansea SA8 4SH 01792 863118
www.pontardawegc.co.uk

Pontnewydd Golf Club, Maesgwyn Farm,
Upper Cwmbran, Cwmbran NP44 1AB
01633 482170

Pontypool Golf Club, Lasgarn Lane, Pontypool
NP4 8TR 01495 763655
www.pontypoolgolf.co.uk

Pontypridd Golf Club, Ty Gwyn Road,
Pontypridd CF37 4DJ 01443 402359
www.pontypriddgolfclub.org.uk

Porthmadog Golf Club, Morfa Bychan,
Porthmadog LL49 9UU 01766 514124
www.porthmadog-golf-club.co.uk

Prestatyn Golf Club, Marine Road East,
Prestatyn LL19 7HS 01745 854320
www.prestatyngolfclub.co.uk

Priskilly Forest Golf Club, Castle Morris,
Haverfordwest SA62 5EH 01348 840276
www.priskilly-forest.co.uk

Pwllheli Golf Club, Golf Road, Pwllheli
LL53 5PS 01758 701644
www.pwllheligolfclub.co.uk

Pyle & Kenfig Golf Club, Waun-y-Mer Road,
Kenfig, Bridgend CF33 4PU 01656 771613
www.pandkgolfclub.co.uk

R

Radyr Golf Club, Drysgol Road, Radyr, Cardiff
CF15 8BS 02920 842408
www.radyrgolf.co.uk

RAF St Athan Golf Club, Clive Road, St Athan
Barry CF62 4JD 01446 751043

Raglan Parc Golf Club, Park Lodge, Raglan,
NP15 2ER 01291 690077
www.raglanparc.co.uk

Rhondda Golf Club, Golf House, Penrhys,
Pontygwaith CF43 3PW 01443 441384

Rhosgoch Golf Club, Rhosgoch, Builth Wells,
LD2 3JY 01497 851251
www.rhosgoch-golf.co.uk

Rhos-on-Sea Golf Club, 58 Glan-y-Mor Road,
Penrhyn Bay, Llandudno LL30 2PU
01492 549641
www.rhosgolf.co.uk

Rhuddlan Golf Club, Meliden Road, Rhuddlan
LL18 6LB 01745 590217
www.rhuddlangolfclub.co.uk

Rhyl Golf Club, Coast Road, Rhyl LL18 3RE
01745 353171
www.rhylgolfclub.com

Ridgeway Golf Club, Caerphilly Mountain,
Caerphilly CF83 1LY 02920 882255
www.ridgewaygolfclub.co.uk

Rolls of Monmouth Golf Club, The Hendre,
Monmouth NP25 5HG 01600 715353
www.therollsgolfclub.co.uk

Royal Porthcawl Golf Club, Rest Bay,
Porthcawl CF36 3UW 01656 782251
www.royalporthcawl.com

Royal St David's Golf Club, Harlech LL46 2UB
01766 780361
www.royalstdavids.co.uk

Royal Town of Caernarfon Golf Club,
Abereshore, Llanfaglan, Caernarfon LL54 5RP
01286 678359
www.caernarfongolfclub.co.uk

Ruthin-Pwllglas Golf Club, Pwllglas, Ruthin
LL15 2PE 01824 702296

S

Saron Golf Course, Penwern, Llandysul
SA44 5EL 01559 370705

Shirenewton Golf Club, Shirenewton
NP16 6RL 01291 641642

Southerndown Golf Club, Ogmore-by-Sea,
Bridgend CF32 0QP 01656 881112
www.southerndowngolfclub.co.uk

South Pembrokeshrie Golf Club, Military
Road, Pembroke Dock SA72 6SE
01646 621453
www.southpembsgolf.co.uk

South Wales Driving Range,101 Port Road
East, Barry 01446 742434

St Andrews Major Golf Club, Coldbrook Road,
Cadoxton, Barry CF6 3BB 01446 722227

St David's City Golf Club, Whitesands,
St Davids SA62 6PT 01437 721751
www.stdavidscitygolfclub.com

St Deiniol Golf Club, Pen y Bryn Bangor
LL57 1PX 01248 353098
www.st-deiniol.co.uk

St Giles Golf Club, Pool Road, Newtown
SY16 3AJ 01686 625844

St Idloes Golf Club, Penrallt Llanidloes
SY18 6LG 01686 412559
www.llanidloes.com/golf_club

St Mary's Golf Club, St Mary's Hill, Pencoed
CF35 5EA 01656 868900

St Mary's Hotel Golf & Country Club, Pencoed,
Nr Bridgend CF35 5EA 01656 861100
www.stmaryshotel.com

St Mellons Golf Club, St Mellons, Cardiff
CF3 2XS 01633 680408
www.stmellonsgolfclub.co.uk

St Melyd Golf Club, The Paddock, Prestatyn
LL19 8NB 01745 854405
www.stmelydgolf.co.uk

Storws Wen Golf Club, Brynteg LL78 8JY
01248 852673

Summerhill Golf Club, Hereford Road, Clifford
Hay-on-Wye HR3 5EW 01497 820451
www.summerhillgolfcourse.co.uk

Swansea Bay Golf Club, The Clubhouse,
Jersey Marine, Neath SA10 6JP 01792 812198

T

Tenby Golf Club, The Burrows, Tenby
SA70 7NP 01834 842978
www.tenbygolf.co.uk

Tredegar & Rhymney Golf Club, Cwmtysswg,
Rhymney NP22 5HA 01685 840743
www.tandrgc.co.uk

Tredegar Park Golf Club, Parc-y-Brain Road,
Rogerstone, Newport NP10 9TG 01633 894433
www.tredegarparkgolfclub.co.uk

Trefloyne Golf Club, Penally, Tenby SA70 7RH
01834 842165 www.trefloyne.com

Tyddyn Mawr Golf Club, Llanrug, Caernarfon
LL55 4BS 01286 674919

V

Vale Hotel, Golf & Country Club, Hensol Park,
Hensol, Nr Cardiff CF72 8JY 01443 665899
www.vale-hotel.com

Vale of Llangollen Golf Club, The Clubhouse,
Llangollen LL20 7PM 01978 860906
www.vlgc.co.uk

Virginia Park Golf Club, Virginia Park,
Caerphilly CF83 3SW 029 2084 9111

W

Welsh Border Golf Complex, Bulthy Farm,
Middleton, Welshpool SY21 9AQ 01743 884247
www.welshbordergolf.com

Welshpool Golf Club, Golfa Hill, Welshpool,
SY21 9AQ 01938 850249
www.welshpoolgolfclub.co.uk

Wenvoe Castle Golf Club, Wenvoe, Cardiff
CF5 6BE 02920 594371

Wepre Golf Club, Wepre Park, Connah's Quay,
01244 822090

Wernddu Golf Club, 49 Alfred Street,
Ebbw Vale NP23 6NQ 01873 856223
www.wernddu-golf-club.co.uk

West Monmouthshire Golf Club, Golf Road,
Nantyglo, Ebbw Vale NP23 4QT 01495 310233
www.westmongolf.com

Whitchurch Golf Club, Pantmawr Road,
Whitchuch, Cardiff CF14 7TD 029 20620985

Whitehall Golf Club, The Pavilion, Nelson,
Treharris CF46 6ST 01443 740245
www.whitehallgolfclub1922.co.uk

Whitehills Golf Club, Brynna, Llanharan
CF72 9QF 01443 225771

Woodlake Park Golf Club, Glascoed NP4 0TE
01291 673933
www.woodlake.co.uk

Wrexham Golf Club, Holt Road Wrexham
LL13 9SB 01978 364268
www.wrexhamgolfclub.co.uk

Index A-M

Index N-Y

Useful web links

Wales
www.wales.gov.uk
www.visitwales.com
www.golfdevelopmentwales.org
www.woosie.com

Golf
www.welshgolf.org.uk
www.golf.visitwales.com
www.rydercup.com
www.golfwalesuk.com

Food and accommodation
www.rarebits.co.uk
www.foodwalesuk.com

Guide books
www.graffeg.com